REFLECTING NATURE

REFLECTING NATURE

Garden Designs from Wild Landscapes

JEROME MALITZ & SETH MALITZ

Timber Press
Portland, Oregon

All photographs by the authors

TIMBER PRESS, Inc.
The Haseltine Building
133 S.W. Second Avenue, Suite 450
Portland, Oregon 97204, U.S.A.

Printed in Hong Kong
Designed by Susan Applegate

Library of Congress Cataloging-in-Publication Data

Malitz, Jerome, 1936–
Reflecting nature : garden designs from wild landscapes / by Jerome Malitz
and Seth Malitz.
        p.   cm.
Includes indexes.
ISBN 0-88192-455-5
1. Natural landscaping—United States.
2. Landscaping architecture—United States.
I. Malitz, Seth. II. Title.
SB439.M34 1998
719—dc21   97-48266
                                                                                   CIP

Contents

Aspen (*Populus tremuloides*) in autumn, near Beaver Meadows, Rocky Mountain National Park, Colorado.

Chapter 1

INTRODUCTION

HAS THE CITY got you down? Do you feel the need to get away from it all, away from the concrete cages and asphalt moats, the noise, the rudeness, and the ugliness? Then it's time to retreat to the unspoiled places where nature still reigns, where you can wander along some stream or mountain meadow, soak in the solitude and be surrounded by beauty.

But all too often, when attempting such an escape, you find yourself in a mob of like-minded pilgrims. And the mob turns the woodland walk into a mall-crawl, robbing the experience of any sense of seclusion that you had hoped to find. Then you feel that there has been no escape at all, that the city has caught up with you and has you once again. Frustration is added to disappointment, making you wish that you had a wilderness landscape of your own, one that could be enjoyed in privacy whenever wanted, whenever needed.

Even on those rare occasions when the escape succeeds, when you do find a corner of solitude in nature, the experience is all too brief, and nagging reality imposes itself on your pleasure—soon it's

back to the daily grind and grunge of the city. And that too makes you wish that a wilderness landscape was at your doorstep.

Some people are able to satisfy this desire. They create just such an environment by adapting some design from nature into their garden or landscape, ironing out the rough edges and condensing the effects. They tame the model a bit and personalize it by adding fences, paths, and benches. When completed, they have their own private Eden—a personal paradise offering a lifetime of rewards.

Throughout the centuries, garden planners have taken their inspiration from nature. After all, there are enough ideas to be found there to landscape the entire planet. The variety is endless, and gardens that are modeled after nature's landscapes, like the models themselves, can be delicate or powerful, serene or exciting. They can be as abstract and formal as a Japanese courtyard garden, or as direct and informal as a woodland garden. They can be as spare and understated as a Zen Buddhist stone garden, or as crammed with variety as an alpine rockgarden.

Of course, there are all sorts of gardens that are not based on natural models. Some derive their inspiration from geometry, toeing the line set by compass and ruler; others are governed by astrological precepts. Some are designed to serve gastronomical desires; others are devoted to serve some hobby or collector's passion. There are gardens given over to medicinals, hallucinogens, and aphrodisiacs. But none of these concern us here. Our interest is in landscapes that serve the eye and mind without compromise. The landscapes of nature and the gardens based on natural models are supremely suited to this goal.

Here we offer a portfolio of such landscapes and gardens in the hope of expanding the consensus notions of what is "natural" or "naturalistic." We hope that this collection of landscapes will encourage people to see garden designs in the wilderness, and to sense the wilderness influence in garden designs—thus making visits to either type of landscape that much more pleasurable. And if the models presented here find expression in new gardens, then that will please us most of all.

IN SEARCH OF THE BEST

How did we choose our examples? Certainly the choices were not made at random. The examples were selected to give some hint of the diversity of nature's landscapes and the gardens inspired by them. So great is this diversity that no set of simple principles can encompass it—one might just

as well attempt to define beauty. So much of what passes as design theory is opinionated dogma, sophomoric simplicity for the sake of specious organization, or utter gibberish. We do not want to further any of this nonsense. Our intention throughout this book is to expand the usual narrow view of naturalistic design. We are not interested in singing the praises of some landscape architect or championing some particular style or school. We tried to avoid any preconceived notion of what constitutes a wilderness design.

One of the commonest misconceptions is that randomness characterizes wilderness landscapes. Want to establish a "naturalistic" planting of crocus? Throw the bulbs backward over your shoulder, and plant them where they fall. Want to design a path? Squiggle a hose and follow its direction when it settles. Want to establish a grove of trees? Heave a handful of stones across the site; where they land is where you plant. Random? Hardly. Naturalistic? Maybe yes, maybe no. Successful in the sense that it pleases the eye and conveys naturalism? Highly unlikely.

In the wild, you can find aspens growing in a straight line at the edge of a coniferous forest; redwoods in a circle around the stump of their long-gone parent; gray birches placed in widely separated, rather evenly spaced clumps—hardly what we think of as random arrangements. A forest might offer a dense mix of different species, as do some hardwood forests on the East Coast of the United States; or it may consist of a single species, as do the forests of the far North. Boulders can form a chaotic jumble, or they can be cleaved into rectangular blocks and stacked with a precision worthy of a master stonemason. Nature's landscapes fit no stylistic dogma, no aesthetic theory, no preordained doctrine of organization.

With such a wealth of examples to be found, however, we did have to place some restrictions on our selection process. The wilderness examples presented here were required to show clear potential for garden design; they needed to suggest gardens that would provide many years of pleasure, but would take only a few seasons to realize. The cultivated gardens had to show a strong influence of wilderness scenery, although a little humanization and personalization did not exclude them from consideration. Most of all, we selected landscapes that engaged us and moved us deeply. What are the qualities that we find most effective?

A garden should have a personality and communicate a sense of place. It should be distinguishable from a raw tract of land, or even from a wild landscape. Its design should reflect intelligence and creativity, but not self-consciously so. Part of the pleasure of a garden is derived from viewing it as a human enterprise, as an artistic endeavor, and as an expression of personal taste and sensitivity. For this, the naturalistic garden should offer an interpretation of a wilderness

landscape, and not merely attempt to copy some piece of found scenery as exactly as possible, an approach that is as unlikely to work as it is unlikely to please. It is in the interpretation that we are likely to derive the greatest pleasure, seeing both nature and the garden in a novel way, expanding and enriching our appreciation of each.

We enjoy gardens that give us some privacy and communicate a sense of tranquility. These qualities are not independent, and the second is hard to attain without the first.

We favor gardens that have the look of permanence—at least the large features and basic structures should have it. We don't see how one can achieve a sense of tranquility or sanctuary without this sense of permanence. In recent years, much has been made of the temporary garden, landscapes that can be changed with one's mood or with what's mod. For some, changing the garden design on a whim is a demonstration of wealth, the garden as a vehicle of conspicuous consumption. For others with a transient lifestyle, the temporary garden may make good sense. But with a temporary garden one misses the sense of growth and development, the sense of value of something that cannot be achieved immediately, easily, or with money alone. The throwaway garden is not what this is about. We don't take the garden that lightly. The great rewards and potential of a garden are not to be realized overnight; it takes time, effort, and care, but all in minuscule amounts compared to the rewards. We prefer landscapes that look like they were planned to endure, look like they will endure, and look like they deserve to endure. It's this sense of worth that goes so far in countering the lack of permanence that many of us find so disturbing in today's world.

We also like gardens that show change within that permanence—gardens that are responsive to the light, the weather, and the seasons. A garden can be serene in the soft light of morning, exciting in the brilliant light of midday, and romantic by the light of the moon. A garden can be scripted to be an elaborate shadow play, or an impressionist's dream in the mist. In temperate climates, a garden can show its most dramatic changes in response to the seasons: the flush of fresh green in the spring, the solidity of form and color in the summer, the blaze of color kindled by autumn, and the spare linear patterns defined by winter. A garden that changes so dramatically with the seasons cannot fail to bring pleasure throughout the year.

To sustain interest, a design must have some complexity, employing many elements to engage the mind and the senses. Minimalist art may be just the thing for a quick tour through the modern wing of a museum, but it can be an awful bore to look at day after day. On the other hand, an overall busyness that masks the underlying structure in a confusion of details can be just as

boring. We like a garden to play like a symphony—a hierarchy of structures—a design that's strong overall and provides the framework against which all other elements are displayed.

We enjoy gardens as sculpture, large-scale, walk-through-and-around sculpture that delights us and surprises us at every turn. We prefer designs realized in three dimensions, designs that invite you to stroll around and to explore their special features. A twisting path that offers a different perspective at every turn, a boulder or shrub or other obstacle that you have to step around in order to see the next view, a choice planting partly concealed beneath the low branches of a tree—all these effects tend to magnify the space and create a sense of adventure and discovery.

We expect a great deal from a well-designed garden, but nothing that is incompatible with gardens in the natural style. In fact, wild gardens display these attributes in a wonderful variety of ways, and so do the cultivated gardens modeled after them.

HINTS FROM THE MASTER GARDENER

Not only is nature an inexhaustible source of designs, but it is also the most reliable source of horticultural information. What grows where? in what soil? in what climate? Does the plant prefer sun or shade? Is it a loner, or would it rather be in the company of others? Will it tolerate standing water? Does it tolerate drought?

You find pine on southwest-facing mountain slopes, fir on the northeast side—that tells you something about the preference of each for sunlight and their tolerance of shade. Aspens can be found growing among junipers on hillsides, although aspens are thought to be moisture lovers and junipers are thought to be dryland plants. We have seen succulents growing within the spray of Pacific breakers. We have seen firs growing so close to streamsides that their roots run through the water and into the sand beneath. Gambel oak is described as a 12- to 20-ft (3.7- to 6-m) shrub, but a 60-ft (18-m) specimen is growing in a sheltered canyon beside a stream in Mesa Verde National Park in Colorado.

Of course, the horticultural information provided by nature is advisory and should not discourage a bit of experimentation. For example, swamp cypress has a limited natural range in the swamplands of the Southeast, but once established it is hardy enough and drought-tolerant enough to grow in Boulder, Colorado, without protection or supplemental water. We also know of two giant sequoias, planted as seeds and each now 8 ft (2.5 m) tall, growing in a vegetable garden here in Boulder. So we look and learn, but once in a while we fly in the face of nature's examples and try something outlandish, as long as the entire garden plan doesn't depend on it.

Stone is a prominent feature in almost all our examples from nature. Plants and rocks were meant to play against each other, and each enhances the beauty of the other by textural contrast, by color, and by form. In the cultivated garden, rock has practical uses as well as aesthetic ones. Stone is used to build paths, walls, stairs, planters, tables, and benches. Stones provide a place to walk and a place to perch. Stones stabilize hillsides and stream banks. The generous use of large stones in a garden also makes the most out of meager water resources. Water is shunted into the crevices between stones, multiplying the supply available to thirsty plants growing there. Stone retards evaporation from the earth beneath it. Stone warms slowly and cools slowly, and so effectively moderates temperature fluctuations. And, as every rockgardener knows, stone provides the plants with shelter from wind and sun. Gardens have been designed using only plants, and gardens have been designed using only stone. The designs that we favor most of all use both.

ABOUT TIME

Undeniably, planting an acorn so that your grandchildren can stand in the shade of an oak is an altruistic kick. But most of us plan a garden for our own pleasure, something to be enjoyed in our lifetime, and the sooner the better. So strong is this desire that many people avoid using trees and shrubs, thinking that decades will pass before young woody plants grow large enough to enjoy, large enough to make a significant impact on the design. This is not at all the case, however. Most of our examples, both natural and cultivated, illustrate what can be done in a relatively short time. Although this rules out a backyard climax forest of giant redwoods, it does not preclude designs modeled after young forests in the prime of health, or even ancient forests dwarfed by site and climate.

One approach is to use trees and shrubs that are fast growing or that show their special features at a young age. For example, aspen and birch can add more than 6 ft (1.8 m) of growth in one season, and they are at their elegant best when young. It is true that such fast-growing plants often pay for these attributes by being short-lived, but replacing them is easier and much less expensive than replacing an old oak, and often these fast growers will replace themselves by suckering. In a natural setting, this process of renewal, in which old trees and young trees are seen in the same stand, is convincingly naturalistic and very pleasing.

Another approach is to do without trees and to base the design on structures, stone, and perennials. Knot gardens, sculpture gardens, English cottage gardens, and Zen Buddhist stone gardens succeed without woody plants, although many of these are not naturalistic enough to be of interest

to us here. Rockgardens and meadow gardens are examples that usually make little use of woody plants and are more nature oriented. In most sites, however, trees are a blessing, and using trees to carry the landscape into the third dimension of height guarantees the addition of another dimension of interest and appeal to the garden.

Finally, there are styles that rely on woody plants, but only those of a dwarf stature or those that can be kept small by proper management. A garden of dwarf conifers is one such example; a Japanese garden using trees that are kept small by techniques such as pruning, wiring, and restraining roots is another. But in most designs, full-size trees and shrubs play an important role, and there is no substitute for what they bring to the landscape.

Careful selection of the plants can give you a landscape that will bring pleasure from the moment it is installed. As the planting matures, that pleasure will increase year after year.

FINISHING TOUCHES

Although an unlimited number of garden designs are to be found in nature, seldom do you find one that can be appropriated as is. There is always the need of some alteration—a change in scale perhaps, or a reshaping of the plan to fit your site, or the use of plants better suited to your growing conditions. Here lies the necessity and the opportunity to personalize the garden by adding the details and finishing touches.

Paths have to be designed, and maybe benches, tables, fences, and gates, all of which gives us the chance to exercise our ingenuity and create a personalized landscape. In the choice of plants, we can cater to all sorts of interests and hobbies. There is no better foil for a rhododendron collection than a woodland garden, and a woodland garden provides just the kind of environment that rhododendrons love. The same is true of hostas, astilbes, and a variety of other perennials. Where there's a bit more sunlight, Siberian iris and Japanese iris can be grown in clumps, maybe alongside boulders or near a tree trunk—much more satisfying than growing a hodgepodge of cultivars jammed together in border rows. Although this latter approach does make a design statement, it is not one that is flattering to the designer.

Alpine plants can be viewed in troughs or in an alpine house, but we would rather see them growing outdoors in a naturalistic rockgarden, where their wondrous adaptations can be better appreciated. Arboretums that feature precisely regimented rows of plants, each row devoted to cultivars of a single plant—a lilac row, a forsythia row, a crabapple row, and the like—give you the opportunity to compare one cultivar with an-

other and so are useful in helping you select the best plant for your needs. Such a display is hardly a landscape, however, and your selection is likely to please you even more in a well-designed garden.

On the other hand, some plants are not easily accommodated in any naturalistic garden setting. Much of the effect of a natural design is dependent upon the harmony of its parts, and the outrageously gorgeous scene-stealer is likely to disrupt the harmony. It is hard to imagine a blowzy peony of the bomb type as something that will enhance a garden based on natural models; indeed, it is hard to imagine such an extravagance enhancing any design in which the parts are to be viewed as serving the integrity of the whole. The same is true of the modern, many-petaled roses painted in Day-Glo colors, or the neo-rococo bearded iris, or the hangdog-headed thick-shag polyploid dahlias, or any number of other over-bred exaggerations of the idea that more is better. But there are so many plants that do make sense in a natural setting, and in fact are best seen in such a setting, that the difficulty is in limiting the selection, not in finding something that works.

So look to nature to suggest the finishing touches as well as the overall scheme. Then customize the design to suit your own desires and interests, and create a personal vision of a natural landscape.

NOW FOR A LANDSCAPE TOUR

In the chapters that follow, we tour landscapes from coast to coast, from Maine to Florida, and from Washington to Arizona. A few examples are taken from Canada and the Caribbean. We compare cultivated landscapes with those in the wild, exploring common themes and necessary differences. The wild landscapes are seen as models for gardens, while cultivated gardens are viewed as reflecting themes found in nature. In every case we describe the distinguishing features of the design and the plants that contribute to its effectiveness. Alternate planting schemes are suggested so that the design can be realized on different sites and in different climates.

We begin our tour with a look at nature's architecture, land contours and stone formations found in the wild that define the composition and give it an almost geometric clarity. Some of these examples might surprise those who think of the designs of nature as random, if not chaotic. We'll visit a variety of extraordinary landscapes in which some naturally occurring structure—a wall, walk, bridge, basin, or amphitheater—is the dominant feature around which the entire scene is organized. Most of the examples used here to illustrate such architectural forms are drawn from nature; because so many examples can be found in cultivated gardens, we did not see the need to picture them. But since such forms found in gar-

dens are often considered to be non-naturalistic contrivances, we do want to point out that such forms *are* found in nature. We also illustrate some forms that would be superb in a garden setting but which we have not seen used in that way.

Next we journey to the highcountry to visit alpine rockgardens and elfin forests dwarfed by the savage climate and the paltry growing season. The garden counterparts of these landscapes offer a bit of the drama of alpine scenery in more gentle regions where mountain goats have no advantage.

The next part of our tour leads through verdant wetlands, sunbaked drylands, flowery meadows, and shimmering grasslands. These themes are becoming increasingly popular in gardens, not only because they inspire designs of extraordinary beauty, but also because they require little maintenance and are environmentally sound where adapted.

We then focus on water features: streams, cascades, waterfalls, and lakes in a variety of settings. Whatever the setting, the scene is animated by the sparkle, sound, and rhythm of water.

A tour of forests is next, some deciduous, some evergreen, and some mixed. They are pictured in all seasons and in all sorts of weather. Some are full-scale forests under national or state protection; others are privately owned stands of human design—small groves actually, but with the look and feel of the real thing.

Then we turn our attention to the smaller features of landscapes and gardens, those special features that take up little space in the overall plan but contribute so much interest and beauty. In the private garden, it is these small features that add the finishing touches to the design and personalize it. Inspiration and ideas for such features can be found along almost every garden path and along almost every hiking trail.

The final leg of our journey takes us through a variety of gardens, each designed in a Japanese style. This is an appropriate place to end our journey, for these gardens exemplify many of the ways in which nature can be interpreted. Here we find subtle and abstract interpretations, as well as those that are direct and simple. These gardens offer a wide range of aesthetic and horticultural ideas that have wide applicability: techniques of controlling growth and shaping plants, techniques of cultivation, and a rich repertoire of designs for gates, fences, paths, benches, and other garden structures that humanize the garden without detracting from its wild allusions. Most of all, these gardens reflect a profound reverence and sensitivity to nature while celebrating the wonder and beauty of the wild landscape. And that, after all, is what kindled our excitement in the first place.

Now let us begin our tour.

Plate 1. Coastal pool in Acadia National Park, Maine.

Chapter 2
NATURE'S ARCHITECTURE

NATURE'S most memorable landscapes feature bold and clear elements of architectural integrity, elements whose form seems planned and not at all random. Often the linchpin of the composition is a land mass or stone formation that defines the entire design with an almost geometric precision. Non-geometric components of the landscape—plants, water, gravel—are most striking when seen next to formal elements. Formal components in turn are seen at their best when set off by freeform shapes. Where both formal and random elements are found, a tension is created that is visually exciting. Nature employs this type of design in a variety of environments, and we never cease to be fascinated by it.

Yet, in the minds of many, a "natural design" is one that shows no order and has no architectural components. True, nature does offer such impoverished landscapes—vast stretches of barren desert, impenetrable jungle thickets, ice-locked arctic wastelands—but these are not the ones we enjoy visiting, and these are not the ones we turn to in search of inspiration for our garden designs. This is not to say that all revered garden styles show a strong organizational motif. Cottage gardens in the English tradition often have unbridled exuberance as their primary theme, a theme that masks any underpinning of geometric or architectural order. But without a unifying component, without a defining framework, it is difficult to distinguish one such garden from another, and it is often the cottage and not the garden that lingers in memory. Without strong unifying elements and distinctive highlights, a garden, like a painting, sculpture, or musical composition, soon becomes tedious. The whole is not stronger than its parts; indeed, it is nothing more than a collection of its parts.

The eye wants more over the long run. It wants structure to anchor the design. Color is not enough: a field of orange poppies set against a blue sky is a visual blast, but hardly a garden of lasting interest, even if the color scheme could be made to last. Line alone is not enough: the pattern of a deciduated stand of closely packed aspens can be starkly elegant against a winter sky, a joy for three or four months, but fortunately spring will come and repaint the canvas. How many painters of the color-field persuasion do you remember? How many works of op-art can you recall, even if the migraine they caused may still linger on? In all the arts, structure is what makes a lasting impression, the architectural elements that define the overall design. In nature, architectural features of extraordinary beauty are common enough to provide all the inspiration we need to add structure to our garden designs.

Of course, not all of nature's architectural features are suitable for translation to a garden. Size and scale are major considerations. The slab-sided towers that border Park Avenue Trail in Arches National Park, or the monoliths of Monument Valley, or the stone chessman that populate Bryce Canyon cannot be scaled down without trivializing them to the level of a model railroad—cute, but no longer impressive. However, some structures that are much too large to be duplicated in size in any garden, or much too small to make a significant impact, possess a certain formal cohesion that allows rescaling without a loss of impact. (We have described a few of these, but most of our examples need no rescaling to make them suitable for gardens.)

There is another constraint that governs the adaptability of a design: a feature might be imposing because of its surroundings. Australia's Ayers Rock rises out of a flat wasteland to reign indisputably as the main attraction in that otherwise flat and forsaken part of the country. Place it in Arches National Park or Monument Valley and only its size will prevent it from being totally ignored. Place a scaled-down version of it in your backyard and you will want to ignore it totally. But again, so many examples are clearly applicable to garden design that Ayers Rock can be left to be enjoyed where nature put it.

In this chapter, we will visit landscapes in the wild that feature stone walls and staircases, planters and partitions, pools and amphitheaters. All the examples presented possess a coherence and precision of design that makes them so memorable when seen in nature, and so are suitable for transference to a garden. Our search for examples of nature's architecture led us from sea level to mountain top, and from coast to coast. Our first stop is in New Hampshire.

Colosseum Falls

We sat at the edge of the stone basin and stared across its 20-ft (6-m) diameter, transfixed by the play of water tumbling over the far rim in a dozen silvery ribbons and then cascading down a perfect stone staircase to the emerald pool in the basin's lap. The precision of it all—the intricate placement of the stone, the radial symmetry of the basin, the conveniently placed benches comprising the rim—all so perfect, so logical, so geometrically elegant.

No, we were not on the grounds of some grand private estate, and what we were looking at was not the masterpiece of some great architect. We were on the Arethusa Falls Trail in New Hampshire's Franconia Notch State Park, and the object of our rapt attention was Colosseum Falls (Plate 2). The precisely stepped cascades, the reflecting pool, and the circular basin were completely the work of nature.

We have visited Colosseum Falls several times, and with each visit the pleasure it gives us is multiplied. We never tire of watching the play of the water over the steps, we continue to marvel at

Plate 2. Colosseum Falls, off Arethusa Falls Trail, Franconia Notch State Park, New Hampshire.

the Colosseum-like geometry of the basin, and we never fail to appreciate the choice seating. Only the location of the falls irks us—it's too far away, and we would like to enjoy it far more often.

We have seen larger and more complicated pools and falls in public gardens and in private gardens, so we have no doubt that Colosseum Falls can be approximated in such settings. Nature made the model out of blocks of stone, and blocks of stone could be used to make a domesticated version. Cast stone or concrete faced with stone also could be used instead.

However, if the terraces that wrap around the basin are to serve as benches, the size of the structure cannot be reduced arbitrarily. If this is not a requirement, then we can imagine a version no more than 10 ft (3 m) across. Even at that modest size, care would be needed to integrate the falls into the landscape. Otherwise, the rest of the garden will be reduced to playing a supporting role; the falls will steal the scene—it is that marvelous.

Coastal Pools

Even the coast of Maine's Acadia National Park, heroically rugged, battered and scarred by raging seas, provides all sorts of landscape ideas. Models for stone terraces, walls, even tables and benches are easy to find. And where inland water makes its way to the sea, or where the ocean has intruded inland, one finds small pools of extraordinary beauty, perfectly suited for a garden. What gives these features their unique appeal is the rock formations that cradle the water. The water itself occupies only a small part of the design and offers little motion to capture our attention.

Here we visit two such pools in Acadia National Park (Plates 1 and 3). Each pool fills a granite basin about 5 ft (1.5 m) wide, and each is backed by a wall of granite. It is the stone architecture of the pools that captures our attention. One would think that the stone would miniaturize the pools to puddles. Not so! Instead, the pools are showcased in the granite, set up as something very special, like jewels in a protective display case. There is nothing precious about the presentation; the design is bold, direct, and simple, characterized by a clean-cut elegance and a near-formal beauty. All too often in garden-pool design, one attempts to jam every bog and water plant of every variety into a bathtub-size pool complete with fountain and various statuary. Such designs appeal to us as much as a garage sale. These pools at Acadia National Park appeal to us directly by the power of their design, and not by embellishments that mask form and divert attention from the essential composition.

Plants do play a role, however, adding the contrast of fragile life to the permanence of stone. A blossom, a wisp of sedge, a bit of moss all serve to accentuate the formal architecture of the rock, which in turn highlights the delicate beauty of the plants. It's a perfect example of a small-scale feature with commanding presence.

Again, the problem is how to realize such a design in a garden setting. The obvious choice is to excavate the site as needed, set up blocks and slabs of stone, and join them in the basin with the

Plate 3. Rock-locked pool, Acadia National Park, Maine.

appropriate sealant. Of course, real stone can be replaced by cast stone, or real stone can be used to face a concrete understructure. The plants should be kept to a minimum; forget the spouting fountains, the mermaid statuary, the rubber duckies, and the chest-high canna lilies in sizzling cerise. Keep the directness and simplicity of the model. After all, that is what gives it its strength and appeal.

The Potholes

The center of the small town of Shelburne Falls, Massachusetts, is the unlikely site of a most unlikely waterscape. For hundreds of years, the Deerfield River has been at work excavating its bed of rock, polishing and carving it by water-driven silt and stone into a maze of free-form sculpture, all the wondrous activity hidden from view beneath the surface. When a hydroelectric dam was built, the water level downstream dropped, revealing an extraordinary waterscape, both beautiful and bizarre, replete with grottos, flats, cascades, waterfalls, gargoyles, and amphitheaters. This unique and fascinating place is now called The Potholes—such an ugly name for such a magnificent place (Plates 4–6).

The Potholes is now less of a nature preserve than an outdoor pleasure palace, more of a Coney-Island-style amusement park where the beer flows as profusely as the river. A restaurant perches on the banks, and throngs of oiled and bronzed sun-and-fun-lovers ornament every accessible rock and cavort in every pool and waterfall.

Even the mob cannot detract from the singular beauty of the place, however, and there are times in late fall and early spring when the chill keeps the bathers and sun worshippers away, and the visitor is nearly alone in this extraordinary landscape. The rock, with all its variations of color and form, seems almost too ornate to be real—more like the work of a demented Gaudí than that of nature. But nature's work it is, a tour de force in the working of stone and the choreography of water.

Is there an idea here for a designed garden? Most certainly, and not one but many. Stone is of course needed to create the effect seen here, and stone of a special character. Short of a midnight excursion to Shelburne Falls with crane, block, and tackle, however, we know of no place where such stone can be obtained in the quantity and size needed. Nevertheless, artificial stone can be cast in its place and molded to any form imaginable, and color can be incorporated in the cast stone to suit the design.

Nature has used plants sparingly at The Potholes—the rock formations and the play of water over the rocks are the central focus—but the few plants present do make a considerable visual impact. Clumps of goldenrod (*Solidago*) can be seen, and some loosestrife (*Lythrum*). Across the river, opposite the restaurant and mini-mall, the forest descends from the surrounding hills to the water's edge, thinning and becoming more dwarf as the terrain becomes rockier. An occasional shrubby plum (*Prunus*), red maple (*Acer rubrum*), sapling elm (*Ulmus*), or poplar (*Populus*) are positioned for maximum effect, while retaining a look of perfect refinement. When colored by the first frosts of October, the effect of the plants is even more striking. No season is dull at The Potholes.

Any garden adaptation attempting to honor the spirit of this waterscape will have to show similar restraint in the use of plants. Here, the sculptural forms of the stone and the intricate play of the water about them takes, and deserves, center stage. The Potholes is a unique landscape, and any rendition of it is likely to stamp the designer as audacious, blazingly creative, and at least a bit crazy. Are there any maverick landscape architects out there?

Plate 4. Waterfall at The Potholes, Shelburne Falls, Massachusetts.

Plate 5. Gargoyle, The Potholes, Shelburne Falls, Massachusetts.

Plate 6. Tributary at The Potholes, Shelburne Falls, Massachusetts.

Gem Lake Sculpture Court

Sculpture in the garden? The phrase brings to mind ersatz marble molded into Leda and The Swan, the great bird spouting water onto the goddess's belly; or sculpted cupids already ripe for a milk farm but fitted with cute little wings hardly adequate to elevate their cement derrieres; or maybe something more of this century, something of plastic, something like a flock of flamingos in pink polyester. Sculpture in the garden does seem old fashioned, and maybe a bit pretentious. Besides, what *natural* effect can it give, which is, after all, our main theme here?

But nature itself has a penchant for placing sculpture in the landscape, all sorts of sculpture ranging in size from small pieces of wind-whittled wood to giant steles of carved stone. The form can be casual or free-flowing, abstract yet geometric, even representational. There is endless sport to finding allusions in the rock and naming the formations accordingly: Twin Sisters, Twin Owls, Keyboard of the Winds, and all such wonderful nonsense. It's all a reflection of our fascination with these forms and our delight in finding such sculpture in the landscape.

A favorite example is found along the trail to Gem Lake in Rocky Mountain National Park in Colorado. The trail takes you along Lumpy Ridge—appropriately named, for lumpy it is—the rock sometimes assuming pillowy soft forms, sometimes highly textured and ornate forms, and sometimes precisely cast hard-edged forms. When grouped together, the effect is that of a sculp-

ture court featuring a variety of styles, from the classical to the funky-new.

The abstract-geometric style seems particularly well-represented. The strong, clean form of the style is effective both in harmonizing with the landforms and in providing contrast with the plant life. This is the style of Brancusi, Hepworth, and Moore, sculptors whose work is seen to best effect in gardens. It's these kinds of forms that we find in a natural alcove barely off the trail on the way to Gem Lake (Plate 7).

The centerpiece of the grouping is an elliptical slab of rock standing on end to a height of about 7 ft (2 m), the edges rounded, and the whole stone coarsely polished. A hole pierces the piece off center. The story of how it got there could be spun only by a stoned geologist. It could be a giant palette that the mountain gods use when painting the autumn landscapes for which these parts are so famous; or it might be some giant shield tossed down by titans; or some misplaced and forgotten piece of sculpture by Barbara Hepworth, for it certainly expresses her style. But this piece was created by nature and given a perfect placement here, in a natural sculpture court that would crown any corporate garden or any private estate large enough and bold enough to hold its own in the presence of these heroic forms.

Could this formation be the inspiration for a corner of a private garden of average size? We think not. It's too monumental,

Plate 7. Sculpture court: a natural formation along Gem Lake Trail in Colorado's Rocky Mountain National Park.

and to reduce its size would be to trivialize it. Nevertheless, it does remind us that sculpture can be a strong asset to a garden, even a garden designed after nature. What materials could be used for such garden sculpture? We see no restrictions whatsoever; metal, stone, wood, or even plastic might do, given the restrictions on cost, time, and weathering. It could even be designed to spout water, but we hope that it wouldn't. It could stand in a shallow basin of water—but maybe that is pushing "natural" to the brink of pure abstraction. We don't rule it out.

GARDEN WALLS

Sometimes a garden needs a wall—not only to keep our dogs in and their dogs out, our kids in and their kids out, but for other purposes as well, both aesthetic and practical. Sometimes you have to screen out some eyesore; sometimes you need to enforce your own privacy; sometimes you must hold back the earth to terrace a slope or prevent a wall from sliding. Sometimes the wall is already there as part of an existing structure and you have to decide what to do with it. A wall can also be an oppressive feature in a garden, an unrelenting barrier that can turn a garden into a prison. Stack cinder block upon cinder block, and that's what you have: a mini-version of the big wall at Alcatraz.

But a wall, even a substantial one, need not a prison make. The famed stone garden Ryoan-ji in Kyoto, Japan, is backed by a head-high wall faced with rusty colored stucco and topped with ceramic tile. It defines the very limit of the garden but does not subjugate it. In fact, such a garden, so idealized, so abstract, and so small but with so much implied, needs to be cloistered away from outside distractions; otherwise, the beauty and the message will be lost, swamped by the mundane surroundings. This wall is more than merely utilitarian—it's a thing of interest and beauty in its own right.

Nature has built walls, magnificent walls in magnificent settings, walls that can find application in many gardens. Here we sample several of very different character.

Canyon Wall Beside an Ice-Locked Stream

Our first example (Plate 8) is found in Colorado's Rocky Mountain National Park. The winter trail to The Loch proceeds along frozen Icy Brook through a narrow canyon defined by sheer walls of rock. The walls are pieced together out of huge sandstone slabs, well-weathered and decorated by lichen and moss. The richness of line, color, and texture creates a tapestry that is fascinating at any viewing distance. Few visitors to the park have the opportunity to see this spectacular feature, since the trail becomes a river in the summer, and not many people hike the park on snowshoes. For those that do hike through this grand little canyon, it's an unforgettable experience.

The canyon wall alongside Icy Brook is the kind of wall that is readily constructed and will complement a variety of garden landscapes. In many parts of the country, sandstone slabs are commercially available and fairly inexpensive. The slabs can be set into place with mortar over a concrete backing. Although this is a common method of construction, it is not commonly done with style. Our example from nature has a pattern that is rich in rhythms, and it does not appear at all random or haphazard—this is what gives the wall so much character and interest.

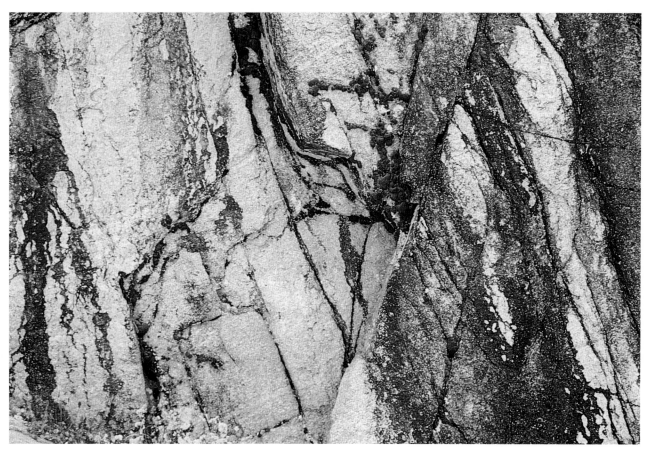

Plate 8. Canyon wall alongside Icy Brook, Rocky Mountain National Park, Colorado.

Lace Rock

Quite a different wall, one much more exotic in character, is found on the hike to Navaho Arch in Arches National Park, Utah (Plate 9). We were amazed at finding it, and astonished that other visitors walked by without ever noticing it. Of course, once we set up our cameras, every passerby stopped to admire the wall. The wall is faced with lace rock—that is what they call this highly intricate pattern that nature carves into the stone in bas-relief. Even on this trail, which features so many strange and beautiful rock forms and textures, this particular type of surface is not at all common. The recessed portion is only 1 inch (2.5 cm) or so from the surface. Desert varnish and mineral stains add to the richness of the design, a design that looks like a giant macramé of modern origin, a wall hanging fit for Valhalla. Yet, in sections of suitable size, wouldn't it make a stunning garden wall? How well it would set off other elements in the landscape while retaining its own special character and beauty.

If one example doesn't impress you with the beauty of lace rock, perhaps some additional examples might make the case. The first is from Cohab Canyon in Capitol Reef National Park, Utah (Plate 10); the second from Larrabee State Park in Washington state (Plate 11). The first shows how nature has worked a single boulder of limestone; the second is carved out of a different stone, maybe schist, maybe granite, although you could easily convince us that it is sand-cast aluminum.

We have no idea where you can buy lace rock, but walls like this could be sculpted out of cement or in stucco over cement. Would it be worth the time, effort, and expense? Absolutely!

Plate 9. Lace rock, Navaho Arch Trail, Arches National Park, Utah.

Plate 10. Lace rock, Cohab Canyon, Capitol Reef National Park, Utah.

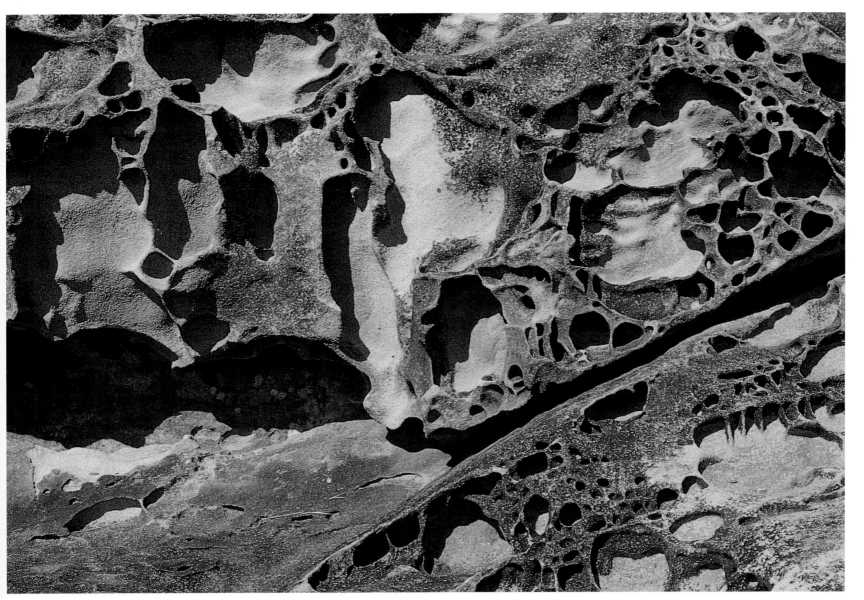

Plate 11. Lace rock at oceanside, Larrabee State Park, Washington.

Forest Path Atop a Wall

The trail to Finch Lake in Rocky Mountain National Park is a joy in all seasons, but it is at its colorful best in autumn, when golden-leaved aspens are staged against dark green conifers and the brilliant blue of a Colorado sky. For the most part, the trail is hardly more than a footworn path through the forest. The beginning of the trail, however, winds along a hillside steep enough to require some engineering. The inner edge of the trail is defined by huge boulders and woody plants that help stabilize the soil and keep the hill from sliding onto the path. The outer edge of the trail rides atop a low wall of cobbles, much like the many paths that we have taken across some steep moraine. Although this wall is man-made, it is in perfect harmony with its surroundings (Plate 12).

This is how we like to see an architectural feature used in the garden. Not as a scene stealer, calling attention to itself and hawking the creativity of its designer, but well-integrated into the landscape and serving some function other than simply ostentation. Along this section of Finch Lake Trail, the need for a path and a retaining wall is clear; the construction is of natural materials found in the area; and the form of the structure is not dictated by whimsy but follows its function and the lay of the land. The path and cobblestone wall are clearly the work of human hands—no attempt is made to mask this fact—yet the construction complements the natural landscape perfectly. You can focus on the wall alone, or on only the surrounding forest, or you can see both as essential components of the same landscape.

A cobblestone wall is just as well-suited to a naturalistic garden as it is to a wild landscape. A low wall of cobbles can be used to elevate a garden path or to edge a path below a raised area. Although building such a wall takes time, the materials are not expensive, and such a structure can be made to last.

Plate 12. Forest path atop a cobblestone wall, Finch Lake Trail, Rocky Mountain National Park, Colorado.

Path and Amphitheater Atop Cadillac Mountain

Although a mere 466 ft (142 m) above sea level, the summit of Cadillac Mountain, the highest point in Maine's Acadia National Park, is characterized by an alpine climate. The Atlantic gales and the northern latitude combine to keep winters long and summers short. What few trees remain in this environment are dwarfed to shoulder height or less, and in some places trees have been scoured from the granite altogether. Even the granite itself was sculpted by the elements, and given the tendency of granite to fissure into blocks, the result is sometimes remarkably architectural.

Our first example of the granite architecture atop Cadillac Mountain shows an enormous slab of stone split into huge polyhedral sections (Plate 13). The pieces are separated from one another by only 1 in (2.5 cm) or so, and the interstices are filled with lichens and mosses. The effect is that of a massive walkway, a path bold enough to receive a triumphant procession. One can also easily imagine a smaller version in a public park or a private garden, where such a path would be just as utilitarian as it is beautiful.

The material need not be granite, and different regions will offer different choices. In Colorado, where we live, sandstone and limestone are readily available and inexpensive enough to be trucked from here to the East Coast for landscape use. Stone other than limestone and sandstone can be used; if real stone is unavailable, then cast stone will do. Techniques for coloring and texturing concrete are so well developed that it can be difficult to distinguish cast stone from real stone. Once the interstices are planted, and a bit of weathering occurs, the result will be even more convincing. In fact, if using a tufa mix of the kind used to make alpine troughs and planters (a mixture of cement, perlite, and sphagnum peat moss), the porous, moisture-holding material will eventually support lichen and moss, making the illusion complete.

Plate 13. Granite path atop Cadillac Mountain in Acadia National Park, Maine.

Another extraordinary structure on Cadillac Mountain is the semicircular amphitheater, about 15 ft (4.5 m) in diameter (Plate 14). The floor is an enormous slab of granite; the benches are rectangular blocks of the same material. The design is so coherent, the placement so logical, one might think that the work was commissioned by the National Park Service and set in place for those evening campfire talks given by the rangers. In fact, so majestic is the setting, one might just as well imagine a sunrise church service being held at the site. But no human took a chisel to this rock—it is all the work of nature.

In a designed garden, back down to earth at a lower elevation, a similar structure could serve as a detached patio, furnished with planters and maybe a table and chairs. The feature is so impressive that even such urban trappings cannot rob it of its sculptural beauty.

Building such a massive structure poses the usual problems and entails the usual solutions. Stone can be used if available and can be placed at the site. Alternatively, a cement foundation can be faced with rock, or the entire structure can be cast in place out of cement. Whichever approach is used, you will have the beginning of an outside room, a room of strong character and great distinction. Of course, when you tell your guests that the room is modeled after one found at the top of a mountain, no one will believe you.

Plate 14. Amphitheater on the peak of Cadillac Mountain, Acadia National Park, Maine.

Altar on Gorham Mountain Trail

We had seen a structure like this only once before, high in the Peruvian Andes in the sacred fortress-city of Machu Picchu: a stone staircase, bench, and altar-table designed by the Incas for human sacrifice.

The structure pictured here (Plate 15)—a staircase, bench, and table—was designed by nature and, as far as we know, was never used in any sacrificial ceremony. Nevertheless, coming across it for the first time while traversing the ancient sea cliffs on Gorham Mountain Trail in Maine's Acadia National Park, we could easily ascribe to it all sorts of mystical and magical significance.

Just as easily, we can imagine variations of such a structure in a garden setting. Powerful as it is, it blends in perfectly with the surrounding trees and shrubs. The altar, as the elements have worked it here, seems to span two worlds of design—that created by the forces of nature and that created by human hands—and so, in an urban landscape, it would be the perfect bridge between the planted areas and the architecture. It is a structure for an established garden, one with large trees. Set it in a young garden and it will overwhelm the design, bullying it into insignificance. In the right setting, however, a variation of the altar-like structure on Gorham Mountain will be the focal point of the entire garden, an organizing influence rather than a scene stealer. It could even serve as a patio, with built-in table and benches. Or would that be sacrilegious?

BUILT LIKE A ROCK

Rock gives structure to a naturalistic garden, and nothing but rock communicates such a strong sense of form. Rock lends a sense of permanence and with it a sense of worth. Rock is the perfect foil to set off plants, and the ideal support for all sorts of water features. Rock moderates temperature, conserves moisture, and is maintenance free. It serves utilitarian purposes in the construction of benches, bridges, paths, and stairways.

The use of real rock is not always practical, however. Suitable material might not be available, or the price for shipping and installation might be prohibitive. The form, color, or texture of the material might not match the demands of the design. Fortunately, an alternative is available that avoids many of these problems. In botanical gardens and zoological parks around the world, artificial stone has become a favorite resource, and often it is a prominent feature of the landscape. We have already seen several examples in this chapter that suggest the use of artificial stone in place of real stone, and later we will visit many other landscapes in which cast stone plays a major role.

There are firms across the country that specialize in the installation of cast stone. Commissions are being filled, not only for public gardens, but more and more frequently for private gardens as well. Besides the cost benefits, the greatest advantage artificial stone has over natural stone is that it can be customized; color, contour, texture, and size are entirely under the control of the designer.

Plate 15. Altar on Gorham Mountain Trail in Acadia National Park, Maine.

Stairs, tables, benches, and planters can be fashioned where wanted and integrated into the rest of the rockwork to give the design a cohesion not possible by other means. The material can be modeled into bold blocks, thin slabs, or whatever shape is fancied; piecing the elements together is no problem at all. Color is incorporated into the cement when mixing, whatever is needed to harmonize or contrast with the plants, whatever is needed to modulate the passage between the surrounding architecture and the garden. Cast stone used skillfully and creatively can establish the theme and set the mood, providing both background and elements of independent interest—in short, cast stone can make the garden. Of course, it could also make a gingerbread house.

Several methods can be used for casting artificial stone in place. Unless the piece is very small, the casting is hollow. The usual method is to make a frame of rebar wired together, although larger forms will require a support of welded steel beams. Chicken wire or hardware cloth is then spread on the frame and fastened with wire. The cement is troweled or blown onto the chicken wire, and then sculpted and textured by hand. Surface paint may be added to simulate lichens and mosses.

Another approach, used especially in the construction of massive features in public arboretums and zoological gardens, is the use of a latex rubber mold made of a rock surface found in nature. The mold is supported by a fiberglass backing. The backing and the mold are removed from the rock and brought to the site of the construction. Cement is then cast in the mold to make a positive copy of the natural rock. When hardened, the cement positive is fastened to the support and finished as before.

One of the most extensive and impressive examples of cast rock that we know of is found at the Sonoran Desert Museum in Tucson, Arizona. Here, tunnels, cliff faces, even walk-in caverns complete with stalactites, stalagmites, and underground pools have been fashioned out of cement. Smaller features too, from car-size boulders to mattress-size slabs, have been made in the same way. So convincingly realistic is this artificial stone masonry that few visitors are aware of its origin. It is from this marvelous museum that we take our examples.

Border of Boulders

Soon after leaving the main entrance of the Sonoran Desert Museum, visitors proceed along a walkway bordered on both sides by massive, chest-high boulders. The first section is modest enough in size to be the model for a courtyard garden, but audacious enough to suggest a much larger application (Plate 16). The red coloration, the texture, and the overall form match perfectly the stone seen in the surrounding desert. These boulders, however, are handcrafted out of cement. Natural rock could have been harvested from nearby, but it would not have given the designers the freedom to create the desired forms.

Once the boulders were cast in place, the plants were brought in, completing a design of stunning contrast in form and color. The

Plate 16. Border of boulders, Sonoran Desert Museum, Tucson, Arizona.

plants are all native to the region. The *Yucca* and *Agave*, with their striking hard-edged symmetry, can be seen as pieces of living sculpture. The tall shrub might be a rosewood (*Vauguelinia*), creosote (*Larrea*), or hopbush (*Dodonaea*); the small one could be fairy duster (*Calliandra*) or a *Salvia*. It is not difficult to find suitable substitutes for the shrubs that are hardy to zone 3. There are yuccas that are native to northern Colorado, and agaves that will survive there without protection. So this landscape can be easily modified to bring the unique sculpturesque beauty of the Sonoran Desert to far more rigorous climates.

Of One Piece

Our second example, also from the first part of the walk through the Sonoran Desert Museum, shows how effectively cast stone can modulate the transition between architecture and garden. Here the visitor looks out from the porch onto a portion of the garden that was designed to be seen from exactly this viewpoint (Plate 17). An enormous cast boulder forms the background of the garden and showcases the plants in front of it. The view is framed by the architecture, and the two are bound together into a coherent composition by the similarity in color and texture of the stone and the building—after all, both are made of the same material: cement. The garden, itself a nice piece of naturalism, is a visual bridge to the desert beyond.

The particulars of the planting need not concern us here, for it is easy to find plants that would give the same effect in almost any part of the country. What struck us as so exciting is the wonderful unity of the entire design: building and garden visually tied together by the same construction material, artificial stone. The porch introduces the visitor to the garden, and the garden introduces the visitor to the desert, each element of the design complementing the others while maintaining its own identity.

Plate 17. Porch and garden, Sonoran Desert Museum, Tucson, Arizona.

Cast Canyon

We have saved the biggest and boldest example of naturalistic stone architecture for last. This one, also found at the Sonoran Desert Museum, is a huge rock wall, perhaps 50 ft (15 m) high, pierced by windows and ornamented with turrets, spires, and hoodoos reminiscent of Bryce Canyon in Utah. The color, too, is that of Bryce Canyon: a deep red-brown. Standing etched against this magnificently sculpted wall, a deciduated Arizona sycamore (*Platanus wrightii*) displays its white bark, whiter and with fewer blemishes than the finest aspen or birch. A few other shrubs and grasses are present, but they seem like afterthoughts in this stark and powerful composition ruled by the tree and wall (Plate 18).

The wall is constructed against a steep slope, so the back side rises only about 10 ft (3 m) above ground level. The window holds a pane of glass, through which you look onto a "rock" ledge that is the favorite resting place of a pair of mountain lions, a strain of cougar native to these parts. So convincingly realistic is this habitat that few visitors realize it is constructed of cement. While much too large for most garden sites, it is a superb illustration of what can be done with cast stone, and it suggests all sorts of smaller variations that would be perfect.

Plate 18. Cast-stone canyon, Sonoran Desert Museum, Tucson, Arizona.

Chapter 3

LANDSCAPES OF THE HIGH COUNTRY

THE highcountry is the land of high drama, a land where nature's most powerful forces have collaborated to forge the planet's grandest sculpture. The buckling of the earth's surface and extrusions from the molten interior built up masses of stone miles high, masses that were then hewn, cleaved, and quarried by rushing water, wind-driven sand, and the chisle-like action of glaciers. By these agents, the great mountain ranges were born. As the land reaches skyward, the climate changes. Each elevation gain of 1000 feet (305 m) is like a move northward of 600 miles (1000 km) away from the equator, until you reach the realm of perpetual snow. From sea level to mountain top, plant communities vary to reflect the altitude of the area. Within a half-day's hike, you can see a wondrous diversity of plants and landforms with the changing elevation of the terrain. Of course, not all of it will suggest garden designs; but every so often, you will come across a landscape that surely does.

In temperate regions, the highcountry is divided into three zones: the montane, the subalpine, and the alpine. The precise alti-tude occupied by each zone depends on the latitude. The montane is the lowest and its relatively moderate climate supports both ever-green and deciduous trees, in pure or mixed stands.

Up beyond the montane zone, one enters the subalpine region. This is the domain of conifers, and few deciduous trees encroach upon it. As we climb up through the subalpine region, the change in climate is reflected in the growth of the forests: the trees become shorter and thicker in response to the near-constant wind and heavy snow. Near the tree line or timberline, the landscape opens, and what trees remain are shorter still and more contorted. Dense forest gives way to isolated stands of dwarf trees. Elfin forests they're called—a term appropriate to the whimsical shapes of the individual trees, though it misses the sense of stoicism and strength these stands evoke.

Climbing higher, we see trees humbled to shrubs, gnarled and twisted by the gales, and sheared to the height of reliable snow cover. In some places, the trees mesh to form a high groundcover that can span acres. This phenomenon is called "wind-timber," in reference to the forces that gave it its shape. Occasionally, one sees isolated specimens in which the contorted form reflects the essence of bonsai, the Japanese art of growing dwarfed trees.

Higher still, above tree line, the landscape hardens. It's all stone and scree and miniature hummocky plants hunkering against the rocks and in the crevices. Nothing can survive up here exposed to the full force of the elements. This is the alpine zone, the penthouse of the planet, where life is anything but posh and easy. Here, where the great mountain peaks gather in the clouds and wring storms from them, only a precious few months separate winter from winter. But during the brief spell of warmth and sunshine, the alpine plants erupt in bloom, staging a dazzling display of textures and colors—a year of survival celebrated in a month-long chromatic bash.

Can landscapes such as these—landscapes forged by such extraordinary forces and beset by such harsh climatic conditions—find counterparts in gardens far below the alpine reaches? Absolutely! Indeed, each high-elevation climate zone, from the montane to the alpine, has inspired a variety of garden interpretations. The coniferous stands of the subalpine regions are the models for the sculpted trees on the grounds of Japan's Golden Pavilion (Kinkaku-ji) in Kyoto. Wind-timber not only inspired bonsai but became bonsai. Some gardens of dwarf conifers follow the lead of highcountry stands. And alpine rockgardens take their inspiration as well as their plant material from those fabulous landscapes above timberline.

As exotic as these gardens are, they also have many practical attributes. Steeled to withstand raging winds, wrenching temperature changes, intense sun, and deep snow, the plants of the highcountry are certainly tough and hardy. Yet, many of them are surprisingly adaptable to cushier climes. This is true of most of the conifers and many of the herbaceous alpine plants. In fact, some are likely to show much more exuberant growth in the garden than they do in the wild, and they may, on occasion, need to be disciplined with the shears, though seldom is there such unbridled growth that a turf war emerges requiring that they be hacked back with a Weed-Whacker. Where lawns give way to rock, gravel, and scree, or where the dense shade of evergreens rules out grass, using these tough alpine plants offers an automatic saving in time and effort. Rock plays a central role in the design of most alpine gardens and does its share to control the upkeep needs—there is no more effective weed barrier. Rock promotes the efficient use of water by directing it into the fissures where the plants grow, multiplying the supply, and conserving it by slowing evaporation. And rock needs no mowing, no fertilizing, and no watering. So these gardens are water-wise and care-efficient, and few themes generate as much continued interest and excitement as these themes inspired by the highcountry.

In our search for garden-worthy highcountry landscapes, we will visit the Canadian and American Rockies, the North Cascades, the White Mountains, and coastal Maine. Then, in New York and Colorado, we will visit gardens that succeed in capturing the spirit of mountain scenery and bringing the pleasures of the highcountry down to where people live.

An Elfin Grove High in the Rockies

Occasionally, near timberline, one finds a group of dwarfed trees, each tree not at all contorted but a perfect miniature replica of its grander cousins growing at lower altitudes. A two-month growing season and a meager root-run cramped by boulders restricts growth to an inch or two (a few centimeters) each year, and such a stand can remain stunted for decades. Here one can see both the forest and the trees, and enjoy the beauty of each in a setting of unmatched grandeur.

One of our favorite elfin groves grows near the northern end of Mills Lake in Rocky Mountain National Park at an elevation of nearly 10,000 ft (3,050 m). The trees found here are subalpine fir (*Abies lasiocarpa*), and the yellow-flowered shrub at the base of the planting is *Potentilla fruticosa* (Plate 19). Moss, lichen, and saxifrages ornament the stone and provide the finishing touches. The planting reaches no higher than about 5 ft (1.5 m) tall, and it grows in a shallow basin carved out of a huge slab of granite. The gray rock provides the perfect foil for the plants, and the entire composition is displayed against the Continental Divide. That's Longs Peak in the background towering to 14,255 ft (4,346 m); the jagged ridge leading up to it is the Keyboard of the Winds. It's a sight worth the climb, even if Mills Lake were not so close by.

The scale of this elfin garden is suitable for the smallest site, and the design would be perfect in a courtyard. However, a garden rendition would require some modifications. Surely, a substitute would have to be found for the granite slab. Nearly the same effect can be achieved by piecing together smaller slabs, leaving the seams open for groundcovers, perennials, and alpine shrublets. Cast stone is another possibility, and with modern methods it can create a convincing effect. Of course, you could do without stone altogether, although this would eliminate one of the design's most striking features. Finding a substitute for the mountain backdrop poses a bigger problem.

As for the choice of plants, all sorts of possibilities present themselves. The main decision is whether to use small specimens of standard-size trees and shrubs, or to opt for genetically dwarfed material. Although the first choice is the less expensive one and will give an immediate effect, it commits you to extensive yearly pruning chores. Even then, you might not be able to hold the size within the desired range without butchering the shape. On the other hand, the extremely slow growth of some of the genetic dwarfs can tax the finiteness of life; large dwarfs are not only oxymoronic but hard to find and damned expensive. However, dwarf forms of spruce (*Picea*), fir (*Abies*), pine (*Pinus*), cedar (*Cedrus*), and hemlock (*Tsuga*) are available that would be perfect in such an application. Using juniper (*Juniperus*), yew (*Taxus*), false cypress (*Chamaecyparis*), or arborvitae (*Thuja*) to create something like the forest illustrated in Plate 19 is a possibility, but it's not likely to be as satisfactory since most of these have an unnatural dumpy contour—too stiff, too formal, and too finely tonsured in appearance to look at ease in a natural setting. Indeed, most gardens that feature dwarf conifers are contrived to exploit the strange form, color, and texture of many of the plants in this group; such artificiality is exactly what we want to avoid.

Selecting companion plants and groundcovers for an elfin forest is even easier. Dwarf potentillas are widely available, and you might consider dwarfs among mountain laurel (*Kalmia*), azalea (*Rhododendron*), wild rose (*Rosa*), *Hypericum*, barberry (*Berberis*), holly (*Ilex*), *Cotoneaster*, and many others, taking care to choose those adapted to your climate and soil type. Finding groundcovers for such a planting presents no problem at all: thyme (*Thymus*), *Arenaria*, *Saxifraga*, pussytoes (*Antennaria*), dwarf *Dianthus*, *Cerastium*, *Veronica*, and *Sedum* are only a few of the most obvious and commonly available choices.

A garden featuring an elfin forest of conifers is suitable for almost every climate zone in the country. It's a garden that requires relatively little water and relatively little maintenance, provided that wise choices are made in the selection of plant material. Finally, since the effect depends so much on evergreens and rock, it's a garden for all seasons, guaranteed to bring pleasure throughout the year.

For a view of another elfin forest in a very different mountain environment, we leave the ridge of the Rockies and travel to the coast of Maine.

Plate 19. Elfin grove near Mills Lake in Rocky Mountain National Park, Colorado.

GARDENS IN THE MIST

With an area of only 38,523 acres on Maine's Mount Desert Island, Acadia is one of our smallest national parks. Yet, drawing over four million visitors annually, it is one of the most popular. Although its spectacular coastal scenery is the park's premier attraction, many inland trails lead to unique landscapes of extraordinary beauty.

One such trail took us along the shore of Somes Sound and up Flying Mountain. Rising from sea level to 284 ft (87 m), it's a mere molehill of a mountain, but the spectacular views and scenery it offers are totally out of proportion to its size. Near the summit, in a mist-shrouded world caressed by mosses and lichens, we found two unforgettable landscapes.

A Dwarf Forest Nestled in Granite

The first landscape is situated on a rocky outcropping on the east side of Flying Mountain, where soft-textured fir (*Abies*) and spruce (*Picea*) are juxtaposed against massive cubical blocks of black granite (Plate 20). Roots are confined to crevices between the rocks, but even there, little soil is available, thus limiting the height of the trees and creating a dwarf stand only 8 ft (2.5 m) tall. The few elements of this landscape are set against one another in striking contrasts, and the design shows a surprisingly rich range of effects in response to the seasons. In the spring, the conifers produce a flush of soft, bright lime-green new growth that glows against the dark blue-green of the old. Summer and fall harden the growth and mute the color, sculpting the scene into more rigid lines and emphatic shapes. Although we have not seen this particular landscape in winter, we know how spruce and fir hold snow in broad plates, layer upon layer, and how dark stone melts and sheds snow—the contrast of the snow-laden trees against the black granite must be spectacular.

The scene suggests all sorts of variations for a private garden. There are many dwarf and semi-dwarf clones of spruce and fir that can be used, including varieties suitable for zones 3 through 8. The design can be modified, maybe even enhanced, by adding a few small-growing flowering shrubs, some ornamental grasses, and maybe clumps of flowering perennials in the fissures of the rocks; see the preceding section for suggestions. But don't overdue it. Keeping the design simple will be most effective in communicating the spirit of this landscape. And capturing that spirit would surely be a prize.

Plate 20. A dwarf forest nestled in granite on Flying Mountain in Acadia National Park, Maine.

Contrast in Black-Green and Silvery White

Our second example from the highcountry of Acadia National Park is found on the south side of Flying Mountain, though it is so different that one might think it's from another planet (Plate 21). Again, conifers dominate the planting—mostly spruce (*Picea*), fir (*Abies*), and juniper (*Juniperus*)—but here there are no blocks of black granite and no dwarf trees. Instead, the ground is covered by silvery lichen, which provides even greater contrast to the trees than the granite blocks on the east side of the mountain (shown in Plate 20). The lichen looks like a layer of hoarfrost, so even in the middle of summer the scene radiates a cool aura. When bathed in mist, as it so often is in coastal Maine, this landscape becomes wondrously serene and mysterious.

Since the effect depends so heavily on the lichen, and since lichen is so slow growing and needs the cool mists for its survival, you might conclude that this design has limited applicability. This is not at all the case. True, you can't use lichen in many climates, but a variety of substitutes can provide that silvery color even in the driest regions. Several species of pussytoes (*Antennaria*) and *Dian-thus* will fit the bill nicely; partridge feather (*Tanacetum haradjanii*) is more feathery and a bit grayer; several of the smaller sages, such as *Artemisia stelleriana*, are even whiter, and their height and coarse texture would give a different effect; woolly veronica (*Veronica pectinata*) and woolly thyme (*Thymus lanuginosus*) are bluer, but they have the right texture; and snow-in-summer (*Cerastium tomentosum*), in one of its more refined clones, is just about perfect. All of these tolerate, indeed prefer, summer drought and lean soil, and all are impervious to heat. On a smaller scale and in a cushier climate, you might try a silvery clone of *Ajuga*. With most of these groundcovers, the maintenance will be minimal.

How much personalization will this design support? Much of the effect is due to the strong contrast between the dark green trees and the silvery groundcover, further enhanced by the simplicity of the composition. It would be difficult to introduce different elements into the scheme and still maintain its integrity and impact. Perhaps restraint is the best approach. Enjoy it for what it is: elegant and ethereal.

Plate 21. Dark conifers against silvery lichen along Flying Mountain Trail, Acadia National Park, Maine.

A Personal Montane Garden

The authors' backyard occupies a bit more than one-third of an acre —a lot of modest size, but one that supports several gardens, each one distinct yet integrated into a greater design in a naturalistic way. There is a rockgarden, a woodland garden, and a hillside garden that slopes down to a stream. This last section (Plate 22) takes its inspiration from the lowest of the three mountain regions: the montane zone. The Rocky Mountains are only an hour's drive from our home in Boulder, Colorado, and we are frequent visitors. In fact, we so enjoy the montane woodlands that we wanted to create a similar effect in our own backyard. The kind of wilderness setting that gave us the inspiration for our garden is in Rocky Mountain National Park and is shown in Plate 83. Without directly copying any specific model, we wanted to incorporate the essential design elements of such landscapes into our own garden.

We set the aspen *Populus tremuloides* against the pine *Pinus nigra* above a groundcover of juniper (*Juniperus*) and creeping grapeholly (*Mahonia repens*). Various alpine and woodland plants put on a show for much of the year. When conditions are favorable, the alchemy of autumn paints the aspen leaves golden-yellow, and they shimmer in the western sun against the deep green foliage of the conifers. During winter, the linear pattern of the aspen trunks is set off against the dark evergreens—a striking study in near-black and white. The garden's extraordinary responsiveness to the seasons is one of its greatest pleasures, always a source of excitement and joyful anticipation.

In this part of the country, where 16 in (41 cm) of annual precipitation is the norm, such a garden makes good horticultural and environmental sense. The pines, junipers, creeping grapeholly, the other shrubs and perennials, and even the aspens are quite drought tolerant. This garden receives supplemental water only six times a year.

Although most of the elements in the design are hardy from zone 4 through zone 7, and many native plants have been used, we felt no obligation to restrict our choices to indigenous plants. Ponderosa pine (*Pinus ponderosa*) is the common pine in the montane zone, but we chose to use the Austrian pine (*P. nigra*), a look-alike that not only is more commonly available, but more importantly, is resistant to the fungal disease that has destroyed so many of the local pines.

At lower altitudes, aspens may not color up in the fall, and they are often buggy, disease prone, and short-lived—not that they are totally reliable at higher elevations either. But there are substitutes. *Betula platyphylla* var. *japonica* 'Whitespire' has become quite popular. Compared to aspens, whitespire Japanese birch has bark that is even whiter and fall color that is more reliable, though less spectacular. Groundcovers and perennials to suit various climates and individual tastes are easy to find and can be used to customize the design. Other pines, such as Balkan pine (*P. peuce*), Scotch pine (*P. sylvestris*), and Japanese black pine (*P. thunbergii*) can be used in place of the Austrian pine.

Plate 22. The authors' personal montane garden in Boulder, Colorado.

A different effect is created when spruce or fir are used to take the place of pine. These formal cone-shaped conifers create an even more striking contrast to aspen or birch, both in shape and in color, although the ground-hugging lower branches reduce the need and the opportunity to personalize the landscape with perennials. But any design setting aspen or birch against conifers will likely make an impact by its contrast alone.

ALPINE ROCKGARDENS

Beyond the subalpine region and above tree line lies the alpine zone, the most rigorous and exotic of all mountain regions. Here there are only two seasons, summer and winter, and summer is a brief and tenuous affair. Gale force winds regularly rake these reaches, and snow can fall on any day. There are no trees at these heights; the only woody plants that remain are shrubs beaten-down to dwarf stature. For nine to ten months of the year, it's a bleak and desolate landscape.

When the intense summer sun finally rolls back the blanket of snow, an entirely different landscape is revealed, a landscape that offers the juxtaposition of delicately beautiful plants against the massive angularity of rocks and mountains. These miniature plants form a tapestry of brilliant color weaving inches high through the tundra, or they gather into tightly knit hummocks hunkering against the lee side of boulders. The foliage can be blue, green, russet, or silvery gray; spiky, ferny, or fat and succulent. During high summer, the plants focus their energy on flowering and cover themselves with a mantle of brilliant color. Soft plant forms and sparks of color set off against massive dark boulders and a backdrop of mountains—no landscape is more dramatic.

With such a short growing season and such severe weather, it is surprising to find so many different kinds of alpine landscapes: from sun-baked scree fields and droughty tundra to alpine meadows and acid seeps fed by snow-melt. Nowhere is the diversity better represented than in the Rocky Mountains, and it is from the Rockies that we sample two very different landscapes. Then we tour several cultivated counterparts, city gardens that have captured the spirit of the wild alpine rockgarden and brought it down to a more hospitable altitude.

Two from the Top

Our first example of a natural alpine rockgarden is found at an elevation of 11,500 ft (3,506 m), near Chasm Lake in Colorado's Rocky Mountain National Park (Plate 23). When not locked in frost and covered by snow, this high mountain meadow is a showcase of water features. Rivulets etch the terrain. Crystalline pools reflect the mosses, sedges, and boulders at waterside. Nearby, the rare bog laurel (*Kalmia polifolia*) and the arctic gentian (*Gentiana algida*) provide color amongst the grasses. The overall effect is soft and lush, not at all what a stranger to this region might expect. Many of these plants, the laurel and the gentian in particular, are so closely adapted to this region that they turn up their roots in more moderate

Plate 23. An alpine rockgarden near Chasm Lake, Rocky Mountain National Park, Colorado.

climates. Nevertheless, several dwarf laurels, various gentians, all sorts of sedges and mosses, and so many other suitable plants are adapted to lower elevations that finding substitutes for cultivated gardens should not be difficult. And in these days of plastic liners, electric water pumps, and cast stone, the water features can be interpreted on almost any site.

Quite a different scene is found at 12,000 ft (3,600 m) above sea level near the apex of the highest continuous road in the United States, Trail Ridge Road, also in Rocky Mountain National Park. Here, along Tundra Trail, we find a scree garden covering acres of alpine tundra (Plate 24). The granitic rock is sandblasted, cleaved by freezing water, and quarried by glaciers into free-form sculpture. The setting is crisp and hard-edged, with none of the gentle softness of the previous example. Only the delicately beautiful alpine plants—mountain avens (*Dryas octopetala*), alpine phlox (*Phlox condensata*), alpine forget-me-not (*Eritrichium aretioides*), stone crop (*Sedum*), *Saxifraga*, *Draba*, and others—moderate the rocky angularity. There is no water in sight, but showers and thunderstorms are frequent occurrences as the mountains corral the clouds and wring moisture from them.

So what can such landscapes offer the garden designer? After all, the scale is vast, and alpine plants have evolved to cope with the rigors of the highcountry. Yet, most of these plants do grow at lower elevations, and their exquisite beauty furnishes rockeries around the world. Of course, the grand setting of the highcountry designs cannot be literally translated to a cultivated garden. Liberties must be taken in the interpretation. The vastness of the wilderness models must be implied—not by scale, but by design. That is the challenge. And the reward is an accessible version of a remote and wondrous landscape, an alpine garden at our doorstep.

Plate 24. Scree garden along Tundra Trail, Rocky Mountain National Park, Colorado.

The Highcountry Brought Down to Earth

A superb example of a cultivated alpine rockgarden is found at the Denver Botanic Gardens (Plates 25 and 26) in Denver, Colorado. Small streams, ponds, seeps, acid bogs, scree beds, flats, and rocky slopes are scattered throughout an area of only a few acres. The transition from one area to another is artfully seamless and natural. The plants come from the high regions around the world, and the diversity is astonishing. In some sections limestone is used, in others sandstone, granite, or tufa rock, depending on the model and the horticultural requirements. The arrangement is so harmonious that the differences in rock type go unnoticed. Even during winter the garden has extraordinary interest, for then the overall design of the rockwork is most clearly seen, and the garden can be appreciated as abstract sculpture. True, this particular garden is located in the mile-high city of Denver. But, as our next example shows, similar effects can be achieved even at sea level.

Plate 25. Alpine garden, Denver Botanic Gardens, Denver, Colorado.

Plate 26. Another section of the alpine garden at the Denver Botanic Gardens, Denver, Colorado.

A Bit of the Highcountry in the Big City

The New York Botanical Garden in New York City contains a section that portrays the gentler aspects of rockgardens, taking as its model rockeries more typical of the montane and subalpine zones (Plates 27 and 28). There is even a stream and a small cascades. High-altitude plants flourish here, located in scree on a gentle slope that provides the perfect drainage so crucial in a location with significant rainfall, high humidity, and high summer temperatures. Alpine gardens in such sites demand a bit more attention, particularly in the planning and planting stage. But what joy and fascination they bring in communicating the spirit of the mountains to those who seldom have the opportunity to see such landscapes in nature.

So GARDENS modeled after nature's alpine rockgardens can be found at all elevations and in a wide variety of climates. Rockgardens can be built in the shade or in full sun; on acid soil or sweet; in zone 3 or in zone 7. Wherever the site, there is a rockgarden style well-suited to it. With such a diversity of plants available for each set of growing conditions, the problem is not in finding apt plants, but rather in keeping the number of selections within bounds. The genera *Androsace, Arenaria, Armeria, Aubrieta, Campanula, Dianthus, Draba, Gentiana, Geranium, Saxifraga, Sedum, Sempervivum,* and *Thymus,* among others, have representatives suitable for rockgardens of nearly every climate. Supplement these with bulb plants such as *Crocus, Galanthus, Narcissus,* and *Tulipa,* and the season will

Plate 27. Cascades in the alpine garden of the New York Botanical Garden, New York.

65

Plate 28. Lowland view of an alpine garden at the New York Botanical Garden, New York.

be extended by months. There are many other alpine plants that are more difficult to grow, and these provide challenge enough to the hobbyist to last a lifetime. The number of species in the cultivated garden is usually much greater than that found in any single wilderness site; after all, alpine plants are usually so small and their beauty and diversity so great that they are irresistibly collectable. In fact, so great is their appeal that the collector often gets the better of the designer, and good garden design is abandoned for a bragging-rights collection.

The initial planning and preparation for an alpine rockgarden takes time and effort, although the rewards are realized much more quickly with this type of garden than with many others. Soils have to be prepared, and rocks have to be brought to the site and arranged. Since a rockgarden seldom has large trees or shrubs, its architectural interest depends on the contours of the land and, most of all, on the rock arrangement. Seldom is the design successful without individual rocks that are large enough to make a visual impact, and such rocks are best moved with heavy machinery. Once the garden is defined by its stonework, however, the stage is set for a four-season show of endless fascination and beauty.

Hillside of Flowers

Perched on a steep hillside overlooking the city of Boulder, Colorado, is a garden that combines sophisticated urbane amenities with the casual grace of subalpine landscapes found in nature (Plate 29). The linchpin of the design is a flagstone trail that winds its way

down to a pool at the bottom of the hill. A magnificent retaining wall accompanies the path and holds back the hill while serving to showcase an abundance of flowering plants tucked into the stone crevices and cascading over the top. The trail's path was originally established by deer, which are now excluded from the garden by an electric fence—that's the thanks they get. The wall and the trail are constructed of Lyons Red Sandstone, a beautiful moss rock that is common and inexpensive in this part of the country.

About an acre in extent, the site is sun-drenched in its southeast exposure. Expected annual precipitation in this zone 5 garden is 16 in (41 cm), and the sandy rock-strewn soil guarantees perfect drainage. From mid-spring to mid-fall, the hillside erupts with one pattern of bloom after another. Both native plants and exotics adapted to the region share the turf with volunteers from the surrounding hillsides, and the volunteers—sage (*Artemisia*), *Penstemon*, yarrow (*Achillea*), blanket flower (*Gaillardia*), tickseed (*Coreopsis*)—provide continuity with the surrounding landscape.

Most of the introduced plants are perennials, primarily species or near-species cultivars that retain a natural grace. It includes plants like coneflower (*Echinacea* and *Rudbeckia*), red valerian (*Centranthus*), flax (*Linum*), *Dianthus*, and *Alyssum*, trusty stalwarts that need no pampering to do their best. On the other hand, a rose bush here and a clump of German bearded iris there toy with the artificial.

The stone wall is a stage for alpine plants like *Silene*, *Saxifraga*, *Phlox*, *Aubrieta*, and dwarf columbine (*Aquilegia*). Here, nestled in the rocks where drainage is perfect, they luxuriate in the sun, creep-

67

ing through the crevices and tumbling over the walls with barely controlled exuberance.

The trail descends through a long switchback to a more formal section—a level area with a swimming pool. The perimeter of the pool is laid out in soft flowing contours and is surrounded by a deck made out of white cast rock, a material that remains relatively cool even under the hot Colorado sun. Wood or sandstone would have been more natural and would have blended more effectively with the rest of the design, but wood can splinter and sandstone can get damned hot. The cast rock is pierced in several places to create large free-form planters. Each planter is an island garden of restrained and elegant composition, featuring an enormous boulder surrounded by thyme and vertical accents of Japanese or Siberian iris. The whiteness of the deck provides a striking background for the island plantings, and they in turn soften the division between the more naturalistic part of the garden and the pool area.

This is a young garden (two years old at the time the above photograph was taken), and parts of the lot are still being developed. Construction of a three-tiered waterfall is in progress. Each step of the falls will cascade into a small pool, and Japanese and Siberian iris and other water-loving plants will be planted by the pools. Even the part of the design that is already planted is in a state of flux, as new materials are added and unsuccessful elements are eliminated. Meanwhile, the battle for turf rights between the introduced varieties and the native plants continues to add interest and surprises.

All this is cared for by one person, its owner and creator, Carol Husted, who manages a nursery and florist shop in Boulder. She tends the garden mountain-goat style, scampering up and down the steep grade carrying soil, tools, and plants. It's grand exercise, she claims, but she admits it can be exhausting.

Here is a design that is readily adaptable to a variety of soils, climate zones, and exposures. The grade need not be as steep—indeed, many would prefer that it not be—and the pool area can be eliminated or replaced by a naturalistic design, one that is more suitable for water plants than for martinis and bikinis. The sunrise-to-sunset play of light that highlights the plants against the path and wall would be lost on a slope with a northern exposure, but one could realize variations that would still bring great pleasure. *Hosta, Astilbe, Primula, Anemone, Taxus, Tsuga,* and a variety of ferns, among others, could be used in a shady site with good effect.

On a slope as steep as that of the Husted garden, one might consider embedding large boulders into the hillside, not only to help conserve water, but also to stabilize the soil and provide places on which to walk and perch while tending the garden. One might also consider incorporating more trees and shrubs into the design, both for the visual effect and to help stabilize the hill. With a design this strong, any approximation is likely to be a success.

Plate 29. Hillside of flowers, Boulder, Colorado.

Dwarf Conifers Perched on a Canyon Ledge

Alberta Falls is a most popular attraction in Colorado's Rocky Mountain National Park. Here, rockbound Glacier Creek forces its way through narrow chutes, magnifying its force so that it beats itself into a froth even before leaping from the lip of the falls.

On the canyon wall is a ledge that few hikers bother to notice—after all, the footing is a bit dicey, and the view of the falls from the trail above the ledge is more spectacular. Those who do step out onto the ledge, however, are treated to a garden of dwarf conifers arranged in a space only a few feet (about 1 m) wide and 12 ft (3.7 m) long. The group of conifers, which includes spruce (*Picea*) and fir (*Abies*), is interspersed with aspen (*Populus tremuloides*), and the entire planting is dramatically displayed against the canyon wall (Plate 30).

These conifers obviously are not genetic dwarfs or virus-induced dwarfs. They are either young trees or trees dwarfed by their situation; limited soil, raging winds, intense sun, and a short growing season may account for their size. Certainly, higher on the mountain near timberline, where these factors are more extreme, the growth of conifers is dramatically stunted.

There is no shortage of dwarf conifers suitable for gardens well below timberline. Hundreds of cultivars of fir (*Abies*), spruce (*Picea*), pine (*Pinus*), hemlock (*Tsuga*), and others never grow to more than knee high. You can choose among colors ranging from pale lime-green to blue-green so deep as to appear black. Silver, blue, and gray tones are always in demand. The texture can be anything from soft and furry to stiff and prickly. The overall shape can be stiletto upright and narrow, traditionally cone-shaped, hummocky and mounded, or carpet-flat and spreading. Such variety beguiles collectors, and the small size of the plants permits them to be massed in a small space in considerable numbers. But here we are not interested in displaying a collection; we are looking for visually exciting and engaging landscape designs. Nevertheless, it is nice to know that such variety is available for serving that purpose.

Perhaps your property lacks a canyon wall. Then why not stage such a display against a fence or a building? Aspen, too, can be part of the design, as in nature's example, or paper birch (*Betula papyrifera*) could be used instead. It's a design that requires little upkeep, although enjoying it will probably take up a great deal of time.

Plate 30. Dwarf conifers and aspen perched on a canyon ledge near Alberta Falls in Rocky Mountain National Park, Colorado.

Sand Forest

On the western edge of Rocky Mountain National Park is Estes Cone, an 11,000-ft (3,353-m) peak of near-perfect radial symmetry, a miniature Mount Fuji. In a region where massifs in excess of 13,000 ft (3,962 m) are common, it may seem that this peak is too small to memorialize so great a man, for Joel Estes is considered to be the father of the park. During the early part of this century, he lobbied, lectured, and wrote about this region in a tireless campaign to preserve it forever. Finally, on 26 January 1915, his efforts were rewarded, and the great park became a national treasure.

In spite of its relatively modest height, the shapely Estes Cone is as dramatic as any peak the park has to offer. The view from the summit is spectacular, and the trail that leads to it is rich in history and superb scenery. The most remarkable section of the trail is within one-quarter of a mile (0.4 km) of the summit. There you enter a small grove of trees, at once strange and beautiful (Plate 31). Only limber pines (*Pinus flexilis*) populate the grove, and they stand far enough apart that they can be viewed as specimens. And specimens they are, each with several trunks and picturesque branching.

However, it is the groundcover that makes this grove so unique. It's sand—fine-textured and pale reddish tan, with a hint of lilac giving it an elusive mauve hue. On this extraordinary surface, each tree has defined its territory by spreading a skirt of fallen dark green needles to its drip line. Although the effect is formal, it is completely natural.

In cultivated gardens, the use of inorganic groundcovers is common; gravel, flagstone, and even concrete are so overused that even when used well, the effect can be boring. In Japanese dry landscapes, raked sand is often used to represent moving water, but this requires a great deal of maintenance and the result may strike some as too contrived. The sand garden on Estes Cone, however, suggests an entirely different approach. Here the sand is not raked and not studded with pavers. The pattern of fallen needles is strikingly abstract and enhances the beauty of the pines. These trees are the only elements of this natural landscape that look natural, all of which argues for widening our conception of what is "natural."

This design would make a stunning garden even without any modification, yet many variations that honor the theme are also possible. Colored sand (gray, brown, red, or near black) could be used to set off clumps of birch (*Betula*), aspen (*Populus tremuloides*), shadblow (*Amelanchier*), or other trees with striking bark. A creeping groundcover could skirt the trunks, playing the part of the fallen pine needles. Placed over a weed-barrier fabric, the sand would require only an occasional light raking to level it, and maybe replacement every few years if it gets dirty. So for little time and effort, a landscape such as this, distinctive and strong in character, can be represented in a garden.

Plate 31. Pines growing in sand along Estes Cone Trail, Rocky Mountain National Park, Colorado.

The Summit of La Soufrière

A jewel among jewels, Guadeloupe is the largest island in the French West Indies. Shaped like the wings of a butterfly, its western lobe (Basse-Terre) is a rugged mountainous landscape of volcanic origin, while the gently rolling eastern lobe (Grande-Terre) is composed entirely of coral limestone.

Most of Basse-Terre lies within Guadeloupe National Park. The highest feature in the park, indeed on the whole island, is the still-smoldering volcano La Soufrière, which rises out of an ancient plateau to a height of nearly 5,000 ft (1,525 m)—a massive truncated cone of solidified lava with steep and rugged sides. Eruptions from the volcano have been recorded five times since the colonial period, most recently in 1976 when the emission of acid gases, ash, and molten lava forced the evacuation of more than seventy thousand people from the city of Basse-Terre for a period of five months.

The most sensational hike in all the Caribbean—no doubt one of the most sensational on the planet—is the hike to the summit of La Soufrière. It's an odyssey through scenery that is at once bizarre and beautiful, friendly and alien. Suspense and anticipation accompany the hiker as the landscape is presented episodically: clouds of mist gathering to obscure the view and then parting to reveal a landscape filled with exotic vegetation set against surreal landforms. Although most of the landscape in the park is covered by dense tropical jungle, the plant life on and around La Soufrière appears more like alpine tundra than what one expects to see in the tropics. Here one finds only low-growing plants adapted to withstand the volcano's constant emission of sulfurous gases and the extraordinarily high annual rainfall of 400 in (1026 cm) per year. Thick blankets of golden moss dotted with ferns, bromeliads, and grasses carpet the mountain, wrapping its fluted flanks in a shawl of pure plush.

The ascent to the summit of La Soufrière from the Savane Mulets parking area is a moderate, hour-long hike with an altitude gain of 1000 ft (305 m). Through a series of switchbacks, the trail ascends along the western flank of the volcano. Each turn offers a strikingly different view of the folded landscape, its ridges and hill crests rising through the fog. The trail eventually arrives at two enormous chasms that slice the mountainside vertically, discharging vapor and fumes along their entire length. From here, the summit is only twenty minutes away, but still a total mystery.

As exotic as the scenery is along the trail, it does not prepare you at all for the fantastic scene you find at the top. Here, on the rim of a shallow caldera excavated by the eruption of 1976, you look out onto a scene wrought by fire and molten rock. The writhing forms of stone, the active gas vents, the gaping chasms and bubbling mud pools still echo the cataclysmic forces that gave rise to this landscape. The constant odor of sulfur and the rolling mists only add to the strange and mysterious aura of the place.

That first view is so astonishing that it will take a few minutes before you regain enough composure to venture down into the crater. Once there, you can climb small mountains within the

Plate 32. Summit of La Soufrière, Basse-Terre, Guadeloupe.

mountain, feel the hot breath of its interior, gaze deeply into the crevasses that scar its skin, walk among the weirdly sculpted monoliths of stone, examine the superbly adapted flora, and explore the strangely serene pools that almost seem out of place in this turbulent landscape.

Once inside the caldera, we climbed to the crest of a hill and looked out at a Lilliputian moonscape. A ring of four peaks encircling a small lake emerged from the mist, a majestic mountain range in spite of its mere 12-ft (3.7-m) height (Plate 32). We walked down into this misty landscape and strolled among the convoluted rock forms and around the pool. Strange and unfamiliar as this place is, its size and exotic beauty suggest to us a garden landscape.

Too distinctive? Too unusual? What can garden designers do with such a singular landscape? Surely, this is not a garden model for the timid. But for those in search of a wildly different landscape design, it could provide exactly what is wanted. The primary vegetation here is moss and low-growing grasses. What really gives this scene its distinctive character, however, is the sculpted land masses. Such a landscape can be realized in a garden on a smaller scale by first mounding earth over concrete or stone blocks, or even stacked automobile tires, using these to lend structural support and to conserve soil. To carpet the bare hills and hold the soil in place, a number of suitable mosslike groundcovers are available from which to choose: Irish moss and Scotch moss (*Sagina*), rupturewort (*Herniaria*), thyme (*Thymus*), and creeping and woolly veronica (*Veronica repens* and *V. pectinata*) are just a few. Small ferns would not be out of place, and even some flowering perennials could be added here and there for variety.

As different as this landscape may seem, it is no more bizarre than the classical gardens of China, where stone is heaped upon stone to create a mountain scene. And the summit of La Soufrière does not require familiarity and understanding of exotic philosophies in order to appreciate it. It speaks to us directly and forcefully. A cultivated garden modeled after it would only do the same.

Chapter 4

WETLANDS, DRYLANDS, GRASSLANDS, AND MEADOWS

WHAT possible inspiration for a garden could one find in wetlands, drylands, grasslands, or meadows? At first thought, one is tempted to join them under the single heading of wastelands. Mention wetlands to some people, and they envision pestilence-filled marshes where mosquitoes rule the air and cottonmouths rule all else. The word drylands calls to mind oven-heat shimmering over a great sea of shifting sand—lifeless, except for cacti, scorpions, and Gila monsters. And in the minds of many, grasslands and meadows are grazing lands, associated with vast tracts of nothingness, to be appreciated only by buffalo and other ruminants. Of course, examples of such extremes do exist, but damning them all in this way is pure slander. In many wetlands, drylands, grasslands, and meadows, a garden design awaits at every turn.

But not only art is served by these landscape models. In many parts of the world, these are the most sensible models, the ones that most realistically address the restrictions of the site. Want a rhododendron garden in Death Valley? Maybe a succulent garden is a better choice. Want a succulent garden in the Georgia bayou? Planting a primula patch might be a wiser decision. Where you can't fight Mother Nature, join her. Design your garden along the lines of nature's gardens that are to be found in the same sort of location. Such an approach is quite likely to be horticulturally sound and will involve less grief and less expense over the lifetime of the garden.

On the other hand, if you live in a desert, you might feel that you have enough of the dry life, and you might yearn for a small wetland garden to serve as a personal oasis. The Okefenokee Swamp dweller might tire of the company of alligators and leeches, and dream of gardens where the sand is not quicksand and mold does not leap from the garden to the gardener at every step. In such cases, it might be worth the cost and hassle to contradict nature's lead, and to plan a garden modeled after examples from the other end of the climate spectrum. But again, it will be nature's models that best show the way.

It was not always clear to us in which category our examples should be placed. We found dry flats of rock in wetlands, water-rich oases in drylands, and grasses in all lands. Some of the smaller features, perfectly appropriate as models for a courtyard garden, could just as well have found their way into Chapter 7 on garden details. Perhaps any criteria for separating themes in such a way must entail some ambiguity, unless you omit worthwhile examples simply because they cause confusion in suggesting two or more categories. Rather than ignore such examples in order to make a point, or to serve specious precision, we included them. Indeed, some of these hard-to-classify examples are among our favorites—their resistance to pigeon-holing only added to their interest.

Now let us begin our tour by exploring some wetlands.

WETLANDS: The Gardener's Waterworld

Too much of it, and you curse it; too little, and you pray for more of it. Water can make a garden or break a garden. Deprived of water, most plants will dry to dust. Oversupplied with it, most plants drown. But what is an oversupply? When is enough, enough? Good drainage and air at the roots are necessary requirements for so many plants that the gardener with water-logged soil might think that the best solution is to abandon the landscape to the mosquitoes.

Even on a site with perpetually wet soils, however, all sorts of design possibilities are evident, possibilities that will bring joy throughout the year. In fact, a great many choice plants will find such a site perfect, just what they need. A short list of such plants includes various ferns, horsetails (*Equisetum*), many glorious iris, and a variety of sedges and grasses. Suitable perennials abound in such genera as *Astilbe, Caltha, Hosta, Ligularia, Lobelia, Lysichiton, Lysimachia, Lythrum, Peltiphyllum, Primula, Ranunculus, Rheum, Rodgersia*, and many others. And don't think that only certain herbaceous plants favor wet feet. Many woody plants not only tolerate having their feet in water, they prefer it. Swamp cypress (*Taxodium distichum*) is choice in such spots; several birches (*Betula*), willows (*Salix*), and some dogwoods (*Cornus*), both shrubs and trees, are just a few other classic options.

Even with so many suitable plants, how do you garden in a wetland? How do you move around in it? How do you enjoy it? Donning a pair of hip boots or waders every time you want to stroll about may not be to everyone's liking. But there are alternatives, and we will tour several sites that illustrate strategies that make a wetland garden a pleasure to work in and a pleasure to visit. First on our itinerary is the famed Red Maple Swamp in Cape Cod, Massachusetts.

Red Maple Swamp

If you think of swamps as invariably dank and dreary, then surely you have not visited Red Maple Swamp in Cape Cod, Massachusetts. There is nothing oppressive or sinister about this swamp; all it offers is beauty and fascination. Seen in early spring (as in Plate 33), the effect is pure impressionism: fragmented light and shadows filtering through a mesh of fine branchlets, spots of color in newly emerging buds, and sprays of grass still sporting their spent plumes. Not deciduated, not yet fully in leaf, the red maple (*Acer rubrum*) justifies its name by the color of its flowers, its unfolding leaves, and the last of last year's keys—a hazy red mixed with tints of orange and tan.

You walk through this swamp on a path of planked timber, barely above the saturated soil. The path winds around glorious groves of ancient trees and stands of saplings waiting to replace them. Occasionally, the path widens to provide a viewing platform, and then constricts to 3 ft (0.9 m) across—a shape as natural as a river, but as convenient as a sidewalk.

Water surrounds you. Slow-moving streams swell into ponds and reform again into streams. Was this the model for the walkway? The water, moving or still, is black, astonishingly black, but clean-looking, clean-smelling, and highly reflective. Ferns are everywhere: ostrich fern (*Matteuccia struthiopteris*), sensitive fern (*Onoclea sensibilis*), royal fern (*Osmunda regalis*), and others lend a primitive feel to the landscape. Sedges and grasses contribute grace and color. And towering over all are the magnificent red maples. Graceful young trees with black trunks stand beside venerable patriarchs, their dark gray bark heavily fissured, some sporting giant burls on their now-crooked frames, heroic in their massive proportions and their scarring. All this dark, massive beauty is set off by a haze of red, tan, and yellow leaf-buds and leaflets in every imaginable variation.

That is what it was like when we were there in early spring. The forest was still open enough to admit the breezes coming in from the Atlantic Ocean, and the breezes played over the dark water, causing glints of sunlight to be reflected off the shallow ripples. There were no flies and no mosquitoes, and the temperature was a nearly perfect 70°F (21°C). No landscape could have pleased us more in any season, but we want to return to this one in every other season. Just imagine this landscape in autumn. Red maple is synonymous with scarlet maple (also swamp maple), and these names only hint at the variety of incandescent colors that autumn bestows on these trees: red in all its fiery manifestations, but also orange, gold, yellow, rose, and too many other shades to name or pin down.

A private landscape or public garden patterned after this model could not do better than have red maples as its main element—a joy in every season. These trees are fast-growing and hardy from zones 3 to 7. So popular have they become that dozens of selections are available: dwarf forms, broad forms, narrow forms, and many cultivars selected for their autumn display in yellow, gold, orange, and a riotous variety of reds.

Shrubs to complement the trees have to be somewhat shade tolerant as well as moisture tolerant at the root. Swamp azalea (*Rhododendron viscosum*), viburnums (*Viburnum*), dwarf willows (*Salix*), honeysuckles (*Lonicera*), shrubby dogwoods (*Cornus*), summersweet (*Clethra*), and blueberries (*Vaccinium*) are all candidates, and most will give a superb floral display and a great show of fall color. To accompany the shrubs, many perennials make fine choices. Silver grass (*Miscanthus*), Japanese fountain grass (*Pennisetum alopecuroides*), yellow flag, Louisiana, and Japanese iris, marsh marigold (*Caltha palustris*), and buttercup (*Ranunculus*), to name a few, can be used as a focal point. But again, don't overdo it. The trees should hold center stage; the rest, beautiful as it may be, is secondary.

Plate 33. Red Maple Swamp, Cape Cod, Massachusetts.

Seaweed Garden

Water, water everywhere—literally, since this is a seaweed garden, completely underwater except during low tide (Plate 34). True, it can smell a bit fishy at times and the footing is none too secure, but it is undeniably beautiful. We have seen landscapes high in the mountains that look like this seaweed garden: boulder fields wet with snow-melt, clumps of sedges arching over boulders, glistening in the sun. We have seen similar landscapes along rivers fast moving enough to deposit boulders on their shores, the boulders moist enough to support moss and algae. Although these don't smell as fishy, none impressed us more than this seaweed garden in Acadia National Park. Even if you don't have an ocean at your doorstep, there are ideas to be gleaned from this landscape that can be used in wetland as well as dryland designs.

The use of inorganic groundcovers—gravel, pebbles, or cobbles—is commonplace these days. These are low-cost, low-maintenance alternatives to bluegrass, the plant despot that rules suburbia's weekends. In most situations where we see such inorganic groundcovers used, however, the stone is put down uniformly, without imagination or artistry of any kind. The only relief from absolute monotony is an island of soil here and there with an occasional shrub or tree poking out—an oasis in a barren desert offering little relief for our thirst for beauty in the landscape.

The seaweed garden pictured here suggests a different approach. First of all, the boulders and cobbles of our example are not the ubiquitous tan or buff-colored stone, but rather a more robust and uncommon black. Unfortunately, commercial sources of black river pebbles are even less common, and when found will cost you the stone's weight in gold; black cobbles or boulders are seldom available at all. So do what the designer of the superb Zen Buddhist stone garden in Boulder, Colorado, (pictured in Plate 119) has done: paint them! Black paint, particularly one formulated to be used on exterior concrete, will weather very well.

Another difference between the typical garden use of cobbles and nature's use in this seaweed garden is the great variation in the size of the stones. The latter includes stones ranging from sand and pea-size pebbles to boulders the size of a bushel basket. Such variation allows the designer to arrange the rocks in groups to provide sculptural interest among the groups and within the groups, a relief from the boring homogeneity of the usual approach.

The most significant difference between nature's design and the typical suburban variation is in the use of plants. In the example from Acadia, the seaweed is nearly as prominent as the stone, and several different species create a fascinating and varied tapestry. How much seaweed should your garden have? Probably not much, unless the site is regularly invaded by the sea. Fortunately, inlanders can find many substitutes. Grasses and grasslike plants offer all sorts of possibilities: sedge (*Carex*), fountain grass (*Pennisetum*), Japanese silver grass (*Miscanthus*), lily-turf (*Liriope*), and mondo

Plate 34. Seaweed garden, Acadia National Park, Maine.

grass (*Ophiopogon*), including the shining black *O. planiscapus* 'Nigrescens', to drop a few names. Some are hardy to zone 4; most will succeed in zone 5 or 6.

A small colony of ferns would fit nicely into the design, and a wide selection of hardy candidates can be found. Would such a garden support a spot of color? How about a deep purple Siberian iris (*Iris sibirica*), or maybe one in white or even pale pink. Many other appropriate perennials come to mind, too many to list. In acid, moist but fast-draining soils, a collection of dwarf heaths (*Calluna*) and heathers (*Erica*) would be appropriate, contributing subtle leaf and flower colors for most of the year.

We don't think that there is a limit to the choices for playing plants against black cobbles and boulders, and this gives the designer limitless ways of customizing the landscape. There is even some pleasure to be derived from such a landscape in telling others that it was modeled after a bed of seaweed.

Reflections

Reflections! How they rework a landscape, giving even the simplest designs a richness of interacting lines, forms, and colors. Reflections in water! With every breeze that plays across the surface, the reflections are animated, and the entire landscape dances. The gentle dance can captivate you for hours. From time to time, you may want to vary the pattern a bit—a pebble skipped across the water will do nicely.

The reflections in our example (Plate 35) are from the marshes of Sawhill Ponds, a small wildlife sanctuary in Boulder, Colorado. The land was reclaimed from a gravel mining operation in the mid-1950s. Water collected in the extensive system of excavated gravel pits, and the surrounding forest was allowed to grow in and heal the scars. Soon beaver and muskrat settled in and redesigned the pits left by the earth-moving machines, softening the contours and joining the ponds. Now a good part of the landscape is a proper marsh, rich with plants and animals, and a popular stopover for a variety of migratory birds. Ducks of a dozen sorts, geese, little black herons, great blue herons, and other waterfowl come by twice a year and stay a bit to rest and fatten up. Songbirds, especially warblers, fill the marsh with music. Great raptors perch majestically high in the cottonwood snags: red-winged and red-tailed hawks, sharp-shinned hawks, sparrow hawks, magnificent osprey, and even bald eagles occasionally lend their noble presence. For comic relief, add to this mix the constant squawking and squabbling of red-winged blackbirds, yellow-headed blackbirds, grackles, and an assortment of other gronkers, and you begin to see how lively a place this is.

Sawhill Ponds is as successful a project of land reclamation as we know of. The site is now visited by people throughout the year. They come to fish, to watch the birds, or simply to enjoy the scenery. A public work that works, to the enjoyment of all.

Can such a wetland theme work as part of a private garden or public garden? We think so, but it will take a bit of taming to do it, even though our example is not exactly a wilderness scene. The general layout cannot be left to beavers and muskrats; as artful and

Plate 35. Reflections in Sawhill Ponds, Boulder, Colorado.

skillful as these engineers can be, it's too chancy. In fact, if the site is anywhere near the natural haunts of these rodents, the garden will have to be protected from their depredations. A system of pools can be constructed using plastic liners or preformed plastic basins. The margins of the liners can be secured by stones and softened by plants, particularly grasses and sedges. And something must be done to control mosquitoes, otherwise the marsh will become a swamp.

The tree used to represent the one in the photo could be anything that is hardy enough for the site, given to a multi-stemmed habit of growth, and tolerant of wet feet. Green ash (*Fraxinus pennsylvanica*) will do if cut to the ground when young and encouraged to regenerate with many stems. Various alders (*Alnus*) can be treated in the same way. So can red maple (*Acer rubrum*), an obvious and spectacular (maybe too spectacular) choice. Perhaps one of the smaller birches (*Betula*) will work, or maybe a shadblow (*Amelanchier*). Once again, restraint is the key, for this design embellishes all that is in it by its reflections. That is its great appeal; don't mask it.

Marsh that Beavers Built

Blessed and dammed by beavers, an ordinary stream bed just a few paces off Trail Ridge Road in Colorado's Rocky Mountain National Park has been transformed into a marshy landscape of extraordinary beauty (Plate 36). The buck-toothed rodent engineers put their incisors to the task of clearing the area of its soft-wood trees and shrubs; alder, willow, and aspen were all harvested for the project. Several dams and lodges were constructed, and the water backed up behind them, flooding the banks and creating a system of shallow ponds.

The ponds are edged with grasses and sedges, and grassy hummocks play the role of miniature islands. The occasional redosier dogwood (*Cornus sericea*) and thinleaf alder (*Alnus tenuifolia*) have been spared, giving height to the composition. Ferns, cowparsnip (*Heracleum lanatum*), mountain bluebells (*Mertensia ciliata*), and other moisture-loving wildflowers are interspersed here and there with the grasses. Mature ponderosa pines (*Pinus ponderosa*) form part of the background, the old trees too large and tough to have been used in the beavers' project. The dark green needles and massive form make the pines the perfect backdrop to set off the bright green, supple grasses. Where the landscape opens to the distant view, the backdrop becomes the Rocky Mountains.

A path of planked timbers winds through the marsh and is so convenient and well-constructed that it is accessible by wheelchair-bound visitors. Besides providing easy access, the path itself is a thing of beauty, its curves and weathered material blending beautifully with the rest of the landscape. It is the only element that is of human design, and the only element that requires human maintenance. The rest is left up to the beavers.

A domesticated version of this marsh would make an extraordinary backyard garden, or enhance the grounds of a corporate or public building, although some modifications would be required. Maybe a slow-moving current could shunt water from pool to

Plate 36. Marsh that beavers built, Rocky Mountain National Park, Colorado.

pool. The hummocky islands could still be a feature, with dwarf cultivars of Japanese silver grass (*Miscanthus sinensis*) in the 2- to 3-ft (0.6- to 0.9-m) range used as the dominant plant, both on the islands and along the banks. An occasional clump of water-loving iris, say yellow flag iris (*Iris pseudacorus*), might be added for variety. Maybe *Primula*, *Ranunculus*, or marsh marigold (*Caltha palustris*) could be incorporated into the design in moderation without destroying its coherence. The striking effect of cowparsnip, a plant not often offered commercially, could be approximated by the bold leaves of *Ligularia*, *Rodgersia*, Japanese butterbur (*Petasites japonicus*), or umbrella plant (*Peltiphyllum peltatum*). Care must be taken with some of these to keep them in check; but impressive they are, and they make wonderful accents beside water.

On the banks of the pools, an occasional grouping of shrubs might not be out of place: azaleas (*Rhododendron*), dwarf shrub willows (*Salix*), and shrubby dogwoods (*Cornus*) would suit the purpose and have wide adaptability. An occasional small tree could be incorporated to good effect; maybe a clump of paper birch (*Betula papyrifera*), or red-river birch (*B. occidentalis*), or a Japanese maple (*Acer palmatum*), or an Oregon vine maple (*A. circinatum*), or a Siberian maple (*A. ginnala*) would make a suitable addition. Even a wild swamp rose, like *Rosa virginiana*, could be worked into the design. As in so many of the models offered here, however, care has to be exercised so as to not overwhelm the basic theme of the design with unnecessary clutter. Much of the beauty of this landscape is derived from the balance of its few elements.

Several different materials can be used for the walkway. Wood rounds, textured cement round pavers, or flagstone would each be appropriate, although a slatted wood path would be nearest to the spirit of the model and might be best of all. The Rocky Mountain backdrop is more difficult to simulate, and the designer in flatland will have to make do with a building or, better, a grove of trees. Still, so much beauty is offered by this model that even an approximation will be richly rewarding. Bring on the beavers.

Grass in the Wetland

Water is plentiful in the Missouri Botanical Garden, and in some sections of the landscape there are so many streams and ponds that it could pass as a wetland (Plate 37). But what a civilized wetland it is! You can stroll to all parts of it without soaking your socks, and everywhere the water seems clean enough to drink. Too well-organized and maintained to deceive you into believing that this is a landscape found in the wild, it nevertheless adheres to nature's canons. The streams seem to choose their own paths, and the banks of the ponds follow casual curves with their logic—no rigid linearity here, just an easy flowing grace.

The network of streams and ponds is extensive enough to allow a wide variety of plants to be used along the banks without creating a hodgepodge of herbage. The well-thought-out grouping of plants preserves a homogeneity within each group that gives it coherence, and sufficient spacing between the groups provides a visual buffer between them.

There can be no finer complement to a water feature than orna-

Plate 37. Grass and stream, Missouri Botanical Garden, St. Louis, Missouri.

mental grass. In this example, several cultivars of Japanese silver grass (*Miscanthus sinensis*) play a major role. We do not know exactly which cultivars are used here, but so many are commercially available that finding alternatives to give the same effect as that pictured is not a problem. The incomparably graceful maiden grass (*M. sinensis* 'Gracillimus') remains one of the most popular. It offers a 5-ft- (1.5-m-) tall cascading fountain of extremely narrow silvery leaves that take on an auburn hue in the fall and are then topped with large but graceful inflorescences that are decorative well into November. *Miscanthus sinensis* 'Morning Light' is even more silvery, somewhat shorter, a bit less graceful, and has a slightly wider leaf. 'Zebrinus' is a bolder variety, to 6 ft (1.8 m) tall, with leaves 0.75 in (1.9 cm) wide and boldly marked with horizontal bands of white. Superb, but one must be patient—the new spring growth is solid green, and it may be late June until the pattern emerges. Even as an all-green fountain of foliage, however, 'Zebrinus' is an effective ornamental. Still more to our liking is *M. sinensis* 'Strictus', with the same striking bands of white, but much more fastigiate and slightly hardier (to the colder parts of zone 4). There are also much shorter cultivars, such as 'Yaku Jima' and 'Gracillimus Nana', both to about 4 ft (1.2 m) tall, and cultivars like 'Variegatus' that have bold stripes of green and white running lengthwise along the leaf.

In addition, many other grasses associate nicely with Japanese silver grass and are highly effective in their own right. Rose fountain grass (*Pennisetum alopecuroides*) is superb near water: a 2-ft

(0.6-m) arching mound of threadlike leaves crowned in the fall by pokerlike silvery pink inflorescences. The bronzy brown leatherleaf sedge (*Carex buchananii*) grows to 2 ft (0.6 m), with upright blades having curlicue tips. Variegated Japanese sedge (*C. morrowii* 'Variegata') is a low (16-in [41-cm]) mound of swirling green-and-yellow-striped leaves. Blood grass (*Imperata cylindrica* 'Red Baron') has an upright form reaching the same height, with the top half of each leaf colored blood red. And there are various fescues (*Festuca*) offering blue-green to silvery blue foliage. All these will add a surprising spot of color, although fescue and blood grass object to water-logged soils.

Several other plants with grasslike forms can be recommended. The zebra sedge (*Scirpus tabernaemontana* 'Zebrinus') resembles *Miscanthus sinensis* 'Strictus', with its ivorine horizontal banding on dark green, but the 4-ft (1.2-m) leaves of the sedge are stiffer, rolled into upright quills. This plant should be sited in ankle-deep water. Big, bold horsetails, such as *Equisetum hyemale*, also complement a wetland, but care must be taken to keep them contained.

In addition to grasses and grasslike plants, a variety of ferns and perennials work well near water: royal fern (*Osmunda regalis*), interrupted fern (*O. claytonia*), cinnamon fern (*O. cinnamonea*), *Ligularia*, *Lythrum* (where it can be used safely and its planting is permitted by law), and many others. However, the strength of this example is due in part to the restrained use of plants. Embellishing it with too much variation will diminish its impact. Keep this one simple for maximum effect.

Grass and Stone by the Water's Edge

It is not always easy for the traveler on foot to reach the shoreline of Somes Sound on Mount Desert Island off the coast of Maine. There are places where the land drops precipitously into the water, and other places where the shore is a jumble of blocks of granite. But access is easy from the Eastern Mountain Club Campground, where a white wooden stairway leads down to the water's edge.

At the foot of the stairway is a narrow stretch of sand, about 12 ft (3.7 m) wide, studded with boulders and grasses. It is all nature's doing, but in one section the boulders seem to have been arranged and fitted together with careful thought and planning, and the grasses subsequently added with due consideration to complete the design (Plate 38). This is a small but striking landscape, highly suggestive of a garden feature.

The Great Landscape Architect surely intended that stone and grass be seen together—they complement each other so well—the graceful arching blades of blue-green grass set against the angular contours of the pale gray granite. Mount Desert Island is built on such stone, and the grass is common along most of the waterways. But here it is the arrangement that sets this landscape apart as something special. Special as it is, re-creating it in a garden setting presents no problems whatsoever, at least if such boulders are obtainable and can be moved to the garden and set into place.

To our eyes, the grass looks very much like Japanese silver grass (*Miscanthus sinensis*), of which many cultivars are available varying

Plate 38. Grass and stone on the shore of Somes Sound, Acadia National Park, Maine.

91

in mature size, patterning on the blades, and design of the inflorescence. Knee-high dwarf cultivars 2 ft (0.6 m) tall to giants 6 ft (1.8 m) tall allow the designer the flexibility to reduce or enlarge the dimensions of the model. The long-lasting autumn display of leaf color and filigree seed heads might reduce the subtle appeal of the design a bit, but we doubt anyone will object. Several other grasses could be used—fountain grass (*Pennisetum*) or reed grass (*Calamagrostis*), for example—but none will prove more effective than Japanese silver grass. As for including other ornamentals, we would resist the temptation, honoring the directness and simple dignity of the original. That is the approach that will bring the most rewards.

A River's Grassy Banks

Adams Falls is a popular destination for visitors to Colorado's Rocky Mountain National Park. For us, the view of the falls is not the most rewarding feature of the hike, however. We prefer the area below the falls, where few people bother to explore. There, the river gathers itself together to cut a swath through a magnificent woodland, which is separated from the water by a broad stand of grass (Plate 39). The scene was photographed in late September, when the temperature is perfect for hiking, the mosquitoes have retired for the year, and the first frosts of fall have worked their

magic to burnish the grass to a rich coppery hue. It's the only high note of color, the grasses, but what a spectacular note it is, set off by the off-white river stones and the near-black forest.

Glorious fall color is a common attribute of grasses, as common in the garden as it is in the wild. Often the color will persist for months, as do the form and the inflorescence, right up to the edge of winter. Even a short growing season can be viewed as an advantage, bringing the grass to bloom earlier and to fall color earlier. But a field of grass in full growth, a satiny sea of green undulating in the breeze, is also a thing of beauty not to be overlooked.

This kind of beauty is easy to come by and easy to maintain. Such grass is never mowed, never watered, never fertilized, and hardly ever treated for insects or disease. Yet, in spite of all these advantages, when gardeners think of grass it is usually bluegrass, that weekend tyrant with the insatiable demand for food, drink, and health care.

Many different grasses can be used to create the effect seen in the example near Adams Falls. The choice will be determined primarily by climatic restrictions and availability. Then the selection process can take into consideration the height, texture, bloom, and fall color. For example, choices for a droughty environment in zones 3 to 7 might include crested wheatgrass (*Agropyron cristatum*) or a tall fescue (*Festuca*). Make your choice, then plant it, sit back, watch it grow, and enjoy.

Plate 39. River bank near Adams Falls, Rocky Mountain National Park, Colorado.

DRYLANDS

The coast of northern California gets on average 236 in (590 cm) of precipitation per year. By contrast, Denver, Colorado, has to make do with 15 in (38 cm) per year, and that includes snow-melt. More than half of the water used in suburban areas of the United States goes toward the upkeep of bluegrass lawns. It is said that the great Ogalalla Aquifer, which underlies much of Nebraska and extends into seven other states, is drying up and that the desertification of the American Southwest and Midwest is proceeding apace. Water rationing is an often-made threat in the Denver metropolitan area, where we live, and a reality in many parts of California. Even in parts of Japan, where landscape design is a hallowed art tied to the national identity, water for garden use is restricted to public gardens. How much longer can we afford to throw water onto gardens that have an insatiable thirst?

Where gardens are wanted and water is in short supply, the dryland model is the only cost-wise, environmentally sound choice. Thirsty bluegrass, water-hungry perennial beds, rose gardens that wilt at the mention of drought are out of place in dry climates. A drought-bound garden that needs a biweekly drenching should embarrass the owner, the designer, and the municipality that allows it. More and more public gardens in water-needy regions are being designed to do without supplemental watering, using plants and materials that require no more moisture than that which is granted by nature.

But dry need not mean barren. After all, deserts bloom, and bloom almightily. Although a limited supply of water does greatly limit the kinds of gardens that can be realized and enjoyed, several strategies have been evolving to cope with this challenge. One tactic is to apply water in the least wasteful way possible: underground irrigation, drip irrigation, and spot irrigation are methods designed to direct water only to where it is needed and to curtail evaporation. Adequate soil preparation and the use of soil amendments facilitate the absorption and retention of water. Mulches and rockwork further reduce evaporation. Most importantly, the proper choice of plants and their proper placement in the landscape can create a water-frugal oasis of beauty even on the arid plains of the Midwest and Southwest. Gardens designed with these principles in mind are called xeriscapes, after the Greek word *xeros* meaning "dry"; not only are they water-wise but they are also care-efficient.

Over the past several years there has been an explosive rise in the interest in xeriscapes—at least in theory, if not in practice. Every drylander is talking about it, writing about it, and reading about it; but few people, even in the regions that most demand it, are tearing up their gardens in order to refurbish them as xeriscapes. Unfortunately, many of the xeriscapes that we have seen emphasize the big zero—nothing, nada, zip, zilch—providing little inspiration, enthusiasm, motivation, or direction for the concept. What often passes as a xeriscape is a hot, sterile, barren, shadeless environment of the type favored by scorpions and sidewinders, but one that most humans decidedly prefer to avoid.

On the other hand, the xeriscape concept is fairly new, and there is plenty of natural dryland scenery that can teach us how to use it with style and effectiveness. After all, nature has been playing with this theme for a very long time, and over vast regions of our planet, plants have had to make the most out of the least amount of water. The result is a wondrous variety of natural landscapes fitted with some of the most remarkably adapted plants.

The deserts of the American Southwest offer some extreme examples. Here, cactus and other succulents, at once bristly bizarre and beautiful, adorn otherwise barren sands. Many of them, bearing names like horse hobble and hedgehog, are formidably armed with all sorts of barbarously barbed lances, spears, and harpoons. But all this weaponry only enhances their appeal and accentuates the silky extravagance of their blossoms. Such is the variety of shapes, sizes, and colors that many a would-be landscape designer has been seduced into becoming a rabid collector of cacti and other succulents. Here, however, we are interested in garden design and not in plant collecting.

Of course, dryland landscapes are not limited to cactus and succulents. There are all sorts of drought-tolerant plants, from minute groundcovers to full-size trees, enough variety to create landscapes that provide yearlong interest, dramatic seasonal change, and merciful shade even in those regions that most warrant the xeriscape approach. Many examples found in nature and under cultivation point the way.

The Cultivated Desert

A scene from the cactus and succulent collection in the glasshouse of the Brooklyn Botanic Garden, New York, illustrates the use of cactus and succulents in a landscape setting (Plate 40)—a bit of dryland design at its best. Here the plants have been grown to specimen size and arranged like sculpture in a sculpture court. Form, color, and texture were carefully considered, and each plant or group of plants is set off to full advantage. The designer was able to integrate the whole into a unified design that leads the eye from corner to corner, every part deserving attention. Although the section presented in Plate 40 is too small to be a model for anything but a courtyard garden, the spirit embodied in it can be stretched to cover a much larger area.

Like any other landscape, a dryland garden must be organized around strong compositional elements in order to provide lasting interest. True, there are drylands of endless monotony, seas of sand stretching to the horizon. But outcroppings of stone often punctuate the scene, providing a sculptural element that is a perfect foil for plants. The stone may take the form of clustered statuary, a basin, table, bench, or even a staircase, as in Plate 15 in Chapter 2. An engineered example from the Denver Botanic Gardens in Colorado incorporates a stone staircase that ascends to the ridge of a xeriscape (Plate 41).

The staircase is entirely of human design. It is made of natural stone and concrete; the materials are so skillfully integrated that it

Plate 40. Desert garden at the Brooklyn Botanic Garden, Brooklyn, New York.

is difficult to tell one from the other. The staircase sits in the landscape as though it had always been there, providing a ruggedly handsome backdrop for the dryland plants at its base and sides. The stairs take you to the top of a berm, whose ridge becomes a walkway that leads through a xeriscape. It's all of a piece, the rockwork and the planting.

As for plants suitable for such a xeriscape, there are far too many to list, and these days a wide assortment of books are available to guide your way, and commercial firms to supply your needs. Xeriscape is still a new concept, and still presents new challenges and new opportunities. That is what makes it so exciting.

Plate 41. Staircase in a xeriscape garden at the Denver Botanic Gardens, Denver, Colorado.

Private Oasis

The cold got you down? Confined to your igloo by the snow? No end to the cabin fever? Not if you live in Tucson, Arizona. There it's warm, sunny, and dry nearly all year long—paradise, at least during the dog days of winter and the dark damp of early spring. That's migration time, when a flock of northerners heads south.

Then summer turns the tables, and a vast migration heads northward out of Arizona. You have to be made out of special stuff—waxy skinned, cactus stuff—to tolerate the endless days of heat, halfway to the boiling point of water. But it's a dry heat; you disintegrate into a puff of powder, rather than evaporate into steam.

During a particularly bitter spell of a Colorado winter, we joined the flock and flew south to Tucson. Enjoying the cordial hospitality of our cousins, we began each morning at the breakfast table over a cup of brew, looking out onto the patio and the small sun-soaked garden. What a civilized way to start a winter's day!

The garden is sparsely planted. A shrub and tree border surrounds the perimeter, and the interior consists mostly of contoured land covered with red volcanic gravel. The centerpiece is a small, simple arrangement of plants and boulders at the side of a hot tub (Plate 42). Come evening, you have your snifter of brandy, and then jump into the hot tub. What a civilized way to end a winter's day! (If this garden seems too civilized to pass for a bit of wilderness, compare it to the natural landscapes shown in Plates 38, 46, and 47.)

It's a mini-oasis in a mini-desert. The oasis garden is a recognized garden style: a small, somewhat water-dependent planting within a larger, relatively barren dryland area. This kind of planting is all the rage in Tucson. It makes good sense, environmentally, horticulturally, and aesthetically. And such a design needs little maintenance.

The tall grasslike plant in the picture is a fortnight lily (*Dietes vegeta*), about 4 ft (1.2 m) tall. It is an iris relative that offers white blossoms on and off for about eight months out of the year. Asparagus fern (*Asparagus densiflorus*) and rosemary (*Rosmarinus officinalis*) fill in between the boulders. An aloe (perhaps *Aloe ferox*) is to the right of the arrangement, behind a boulder. A mesquite tree (*Prosopis*) and an oleander shrub (*Nerium oleander* 'Petite Pink') set against the wall form the background for the arrangement.

Up north, even into Canada, even where there is an abundance of water, a design like this makes good sense, with or without the hot tub. The size is perfect for a small courtyard or a ground-level patio. It would fit well into the crook of a stream meander, or beside a pool. Wherever it is, it would be a delight to see it from the breakfast nook every morning over a cup of brew.

Spuria iris (*Iris spuria*) or a giant cultivar of yellow flag iris (*Iris pseudacorus*) or a broad-bladed Japanese silver grass (*Miscanthus*) could be used in place of the fortnight lily. The perennials and shrubs to complete the design can be chosen from so many possibilities that it would be silly to list them. The choice of morning brew or evening spirits is entirely up to you.

Plate 42. Private oasis: the Spokane residence, Tucson, Arizona.

Grass by a Desert Stream

Water is not a common commodity in the desert near Tucson, Arizona, but Pima Canyon has water. At the bottom of this canyon, a stream meanders around great boulders and slabs of stone. The air here is cooler and more humid, and the ground remains saturated all year round. Many of the plants found here are not to be found on the open desert.

Hiking the canyon in mid-winter, we came upon a colony of grasses growing in the wet soil captured in a bend of the stream. The grasses were in their dormant state, tawny-hued and in full plume (Plate 43). We don't know how long they had been in flower, but the silver-white plumes appeared fresh, plump, and perfect. The lighting was perfect too, coming from behind the grass and setting the plumes aglow like sparklers against the darkly shadowed walls of the canyon.

Of course, this scene suggested a garden to us, or at least a part of a garden—too small to be an entire landscape, too large to be considered a detail. However, it is one of those landscapes that can be extended, variations repeated in tandem to maybe 20 ft (6 m), and nothing of its effect will be lost. Imagine it as a courtyard, or along the side of a garden, next to running water.

We can't say what species of grass we found in Pima Canyon, but all sorts of candidates are available for the cultivated landscape. Our first choice would be a dwarf Japanese silver grass such as *Miscanthus sinensis* 'Adagio' or 'Yaku Jima'. The first grows to about 2 ft (0.6 m) and the second to 4 ft (1.2 m); both have plumes rising 1.5 ft (0.45 m) above the foliage. The foliage has excellent tawny fall color and the spikes may last through winter. Fall-blooming reed grass (*Calamagrostis arundinacea* var. *brachytricha*) grows to 2.5 ft (0.75 m) with spikes 2 ft (0.6 m) taller, has a pleasant fall color, and is suitable for zones 5 to 9. In warmer climates (zones 7 to 10) and on larger sites, dwarf pampas grass (*Cortaderia selloana* 'Pumila') might do, although it is a bit overbearing in its magnificence and is not too happy with constant moisture at its roots. It grows to 6 ft (1.8 m) and has spikes 1.5 to 2 ft (0.45 to 0.6 m) above that. All these grasses have an upright presentation, in spike if not in leaf. (Do keep in mind, however, that *Cortaderia* can be quite invasive and may threaten native ecosystems.)

Another way to achieve the effect of a staggered arrangement of upright grassy forms is to use iris. No choice would be more pleasing than a white-flowered Siberian iris (*Iris sibirica*) like the classic cultivars 'White Swirl' or 'Anniversary'. The flowering would not be as long-lasting nor as delicate as the show presented by grasses, however. In either interpretation, a dark background will do a great deal to set off the design.

Again, this is one of those designs where adding more gives you less. Part of what we find so appealing about this landscape is the marvelous contrasts in shading, color, texture, and form achieved by a few elements clearly presented. The silvery glowing

Plate 43. Grass by a desert stream in Pima Canyon, Tucson, Arizona.

plumes against the dark canyon wall, the wispy blades of tawny grass in clumps among the rounded cobbles, the unmovable rock, the flowing river is all that is needed.

Before we leave Pima Canyon, we will visit another site, one mile (1.67 km) downstream from this one. Here we find another small landscape, direct, simple, and very effective.

Desert Pool

In the Sonoran Desert near Tucson, Arizona, the heat and dry air have pared the landscape to its elemental components. There is an openness to the scene, an uncluttered directness that establishes bold patterns and striking contrasts. Sand is the groundcover, and rock provides the structure. The plants have the look of abstract sculpture; clean strong lines, rigid forms, and metallic colors all contribute to the effect. It's a desert—a glance in any direction will convince you of that.

Yet, there is water in this region, and water has been the primary architect in carving out the canyons. The gentle stream at the bottom of Pima Canyon barely gives hint of the power it can muster. But when the rain comes, it often comes in torrents, and the desert quickly shunts the water into canyons like Pima. Gentle streams become raging rivers that carry away dirt and rocks and plants, cutting gorges ever deeper and wider.

Along one part of its course, the river has carved its way down to bedrock, and further excavation will be slower. Where slabs of stone have been exposed, water fills the hollows for most of the year, forming pools and basins that coolly reflect the hot dry landscape surrounding them. Plate 44 shows such a place—it's a paradoxical scene, surprising and most welcome.

A few sedges are growing near the water, but the main plant is a yucca (perhaps *Yucca rigida*), a magnificent, 5-ft (1.5-m) tall sculptural presence, the symmetry of which provides wonderful contrast to the free-form pools and the glassy water surface. Our example was photographed in winter, but it will give the same effect throughout the year. Although we favor landscapes that respond to seasonal changes, we found this one so striking that we had to include it.

Could this serve as a model for a courtyard design or an oasis garden in the Southwest? No doubt, and with little modification. Of course, the basins will have to be cast in cement, but that is not a problem. The yucca is a key element in the design, and nothing will quite match its spiky assertiveness; however, a few alternatives come quite close. Sotols or desert spoons (*Dasylirion*) include species that grow to 6 ft (1.8 m) in diameter, and *Nolina* offers several species that grow to the same size. All these, including the yucca, may develop a trunk several feet (a meter or so) tall.

Alternative selections can also give a striking effect, and some will extend the applicability of this model. A green or burgundy-colored New Zealand flax (*Phormium tenax*) to 15 ft (4.5 m) will do for larger interpretations in the Southwest. Blue lyme grass (*Elymus glaucus*), which grows to 3 ft (0.9 m), will do for smaller versions as far north as zone 4. For a still freer interpretation, in zones 4 or 5 through zone 8, some giant cultivar of spuria iris (*Iris spuria*)

Plate 44. Desert pool, Pima Canyon, Tucson, Arizona.

or yellow flag iris (*I. pseudacorus*) might be used, introducing flowers and dormancy into the scheme. Yuccas are available for zone 4 climates, but at 2 ft (0.6 m) tall they make less of an impact than might be needed to interpret this design.

Simplicity characterizes this model—bold simplicity. It's a low-maintenance design that will give you a sampling of an unusual bit of desert scenery. Now there's a warm thought for you northerners, although under a foot or two of snow, the effect might be less than convincing.

Desert Teddy Bears

Teddy-bear cholla: it's chubby, it's cute, but it's not for cuddling. This desert teddy is replete with claws and teeth. It's a cactus, as fiercely armed as any, with stout glistening white barbed spines deployed over most of its plump little body. See this teddy-bear side-lit or back-lit and the spines reflect a silvery sheen that makes the plant appear to be covered with fur. Under these conditions the entire plant seems to glow—intriguing and seemingly benign. Look, but don't touch!

Teddy-bear cholla (*Opuntia bigelovii*) is common in the deserts of Arizona, and it is also common in cultivation. Our favorite example of this plant being used as the dominant feature in a naturalistic garden is at the Sonoran Desert Museum in Tucson (Plate 45). Here, on a rock-studded hillside, the teddy-bears provide the main organizing theme; *Yucca* and brittle bush (*Encelia farinosa*) were all that was needed to complete the design. When we photographed the planting in mid-winter, the brittle bush was already preparing to set its tall-stemmed clusters of yellow daisies; it's a show that reaches its peak in February and continues through March. A few taller plants ride the crest of the hill, just out of view of the camera: ocotillo (*Fouquieria splendens*), *Pedilanthus macrocarpus*, and some taller cactus.

All these plants are native to the Arizona desert and have limited cold tolerance. But what if you wanted such a landscape further north? Yuccas of several species can be found even in Montana. There are some splendid hardy cacti as well, although none that we know of has both the size and striking spination of the teddy-bear. One might have to do with a frosty-leaved shrub as a substitute; maybe redberry mahonia (*Mahonia haematocarpa*), or dwarf *Buddleia*, or silver buffaloberry (*Shepherdia argentea*), or even a dwarf willow (*Salix*) would be suitable. The brittle bush could be replaced by some silver-leaved salvia; but if the leaf color is not important, one can use tickseed (*Coreopsis*), a choice that would give you yellow daisies throughout the summer.

This natural design has a tight composition, and we do not think that it can be stretched to cover a large area. But for a courtyard, or an indoor planting under a skylight, it is hard to imagine a more striking design. And maintenance would present no problem at all, provided that the gardener has a suit of armor.

Plate 45. Teddy-bear cholla (*Opuntia bigelovii*), Sonoran Desert Museum, Tucson, Arizona.

Water Garden in the High Dryland

The most popular hikes in Tucson, Arizona, are found in Sabino Canyon State Park, in the Santa Catalina Mountains. There are trails that lead to mountain summits, trails that meander along high ridges, and trails that lead into upland desert. But most popular of all is the trail to Seven Falls. This trail takes you through a canyon filled with magnificent scenery on all sides. Straight ahead, seen through the cleft of the canyon, is Mount Lemmon. The steep canyon walls are studded with succulents and cacti. Dwarfing the others are giant saguaros (*Carnegiea gigantea*), positioned like a bristly and bizarre honor guard watching over your journey. For more than half the trip, you hike beside a river, crossing it seven times on your way to Seven Falls. Then a series of switchbacks takes you up the canyon wall and away from the river, though you can still hear the water and occasionally catch a glimpse of it far below you. The views of the opposite wall and back through the mouth of the canyon to the desert flatlands are magnificent, but what lies ahead is even more spectacular. You don't see the destination until you are almost there.

Rock-locked into the mountainside, water falls in seven steps from basin to basin, finally spreading out into a system of large pools joined by shallow streams, the whole configuration carved out of enormous slabs of stone. The lowest pool feeds the last waterfall, which drops into the river that we followed upstream. During the driest part of the season, the falls may dry to a trickle, but the turquoise pools will still be here, diminished a bit in size but not in appeal.

The main pool backs right up to the canyon wall. To the side are several large boulders, clumps of tall grass, a small shrub, and a stunted tree. The pool and the planting are well-lit for most of the day, but the canyon that forms the backdrop remains in deep shade (Plate 46). It's a scene of simple drama: bold and beautiful, yet seldom noticed, except by those looking for a place to spread out lunch.

Why doesn't this spot draw the attention it deserves? Probably because it's only a small-size treasure surrounded by spectacular scenery on a grand scale. And it comes at the end of a 2.3-mile (3.8-km) walk that is exhausting, not for its physical difficulty, but for the sensory overload caused by all the wonderful sights seen along the way. We don't mind that this scene goes unnoticed, since it gave us a chance, in mid-winter, to experience it without a mob competing for a view or a lunch spot. In this near seclusion, we could enjoy the intimate quality of the place, and get a sense of what it would be like as a garden.

Uncluttered though it is, the scene has enough elements to interact with the seasons, bringing subtle changes throughout the year. The grass goes from summer green to winter tan, sporting its feathery seed plumes in the interim. The trees and shrubs deciduate, but not before a show of fall color—not a blast of color, but enough to mark the occasion.

Plate 46. Water garden in the high dryland of Sabino Canyon State Park, Tucson, Arizona.

A garden version of this landscape is easy enough to imagine. The pool basin would have to be cast out of cement and then finished to look like stone. The boulders at the side could be hauled in, or they too could be cast and finished on site. The water could be tinted turquoise using dyes on the market for that purpose. The plants present no problem whatsoever; substitutes are available for every climate. The dark backdrop to set it all off might be the side of a building, a tall fence or wall, or even a grove of dark evergreens, say yew (*Taxus*) or pine (*Pinus*). Of course, if the garden backs onto a canyon wall facing north, that would be ideal, but even without a backdrop, this small arrangement would make an outstanding garden feature.

And there are other attributes that recommend this model. Low demands on water is one: keep the pool filled, and supply the few plants with the little amount they need. Low maintenance is another: tidy it up a bit after leaf-fall and again before spring; do the minimal bit of pruning needed to maintain the size and shape of the trees and shrubs, and that's about it. Then, relax and enjoy.

Desert Sycamore

Seven Falls Trail in Sabino Canyon State Park in Tucson offers an entire portfolio of superb landscapes, many of which suggest gardens. Some are suitable for estate-size lots, and some can be nicely represented in a courtyard. Between the sixth and seventh crossing of the river on the way to Seven Falls, the water course is defined more by huge slabs of stone than by the jumbles of boulders that

you see nearer the start of the trail. Resting on the slabs of stone are blocks and boulders of the same material. The forms tend to be flat sided, yet the corners and edges are rounded. The color, too, is exceptional: pale blue-gray, with occasional dark streaks and bold bands of white. In mid-winter's light, the water runs black through the canyon, providing a stunning foil for the rock.

In this setting, right by the water's edge, a magnificent Arizona sycamore (*Platanus wrightii*) holds court (Plate 47). Multi-stemmed and white barked, it stands out in high contrast against the dark shadows of the cliff behind it. Graceful and majestic, the tree seems to have come from a different place, a place far from the searing heat of the Arizona desert. But it's native here, and in spite of its large maple-shaped leaves, it is well-adapted to heat and drought, although it prefers the wetter bottomlands.

This is not a large-scale design, and it cannot be arbitrarily stretched to fill a large site. Its power and appeal reside in its compactness, in the way the single tree dominates the scene. For a small suburban lot, or a corporate courtyard, this landscape might be just the model. Unlike almost all our other examples, the effectiveness of this one depends primarily on a single element—its magnificent centerpiece, the tree, stands alone—and little else is needed. But short shrubs, ornamental grasses, or even a few perennials might be added without destroying the effect.

Arizona sycamore is a popular landscape tree in and around Tucson. Not only is the bark stunning, but the bold maple-shaped foliage is a welcome change from the wispy-leaved insubstantial trees that one usually associates with desert flora. This tree offers

Plate 47. Arizona sycamore (*Platanus wrightii*) along Seven Falls Trail in Sabino Canyon State Park, Tucson, Arizona.

real shade, a true blessing in a region of blazing heat and sunshine. Late in the season, it even gives some fall color, a pleasant soft yellow. Sycamores for northern climates are available, but they grow to monstrous size, with a single bole, and with none of the grace of the Arizona sycamore. Fortunately, there are much better choices that will serve the same role further north. *Stewartia* offers several candidates; crapemyrtle (*Lagerstroemia*) in a larger variety might do; and, of course, birch (*Betula*) is a good possibility. They may not communicate the sense of a proper dryland, but neither does the Arizona sycamore. And who will quibble when the effect is so beautiful, so readily realized, and so easily maintained.

GRASSLANDS AND MEADOWS

When is a meadow a grassland? Almost always, since grasses are among the most successful plants on the planet, with a penchant for colonizing open areas. When plants other than grasses are the main attraction, we tend to call the area a meadow; and when grasses are the main feature, we consider it a grassland, even though the grasses do not uniformly blanket the area. The two types of landscapes are not mutually exclusive, however, and we often ignore the distinctions.

Autumn is a high point for many grasses. They change to shades of tan, some to silky blond, others to russet; some even approach orange, a hue rather boisterous in a family of plants noted more for their subdued beauty. Many are prized for their fall plumes, airy and feathery panicles of seed striking enough to be used alone in dry flower arrangements, modest enough to complement and tone down the more brazen flowers in a bouquet. When left on the plant, the seed heads of many species will hold through winter, even in climates with significant snowfall, and during these dreary days they are likely to be focal points in the landscape. For those species that finally die back, spring may be their least impressive season. Yet there are those that enter the new season with their brightest show of color. Summer has them growing to full size and defining their form: billowing swirls (some *Carex*), cascading fountains (*Pennisetum* and *Miscanthus*), emphatically upright (some *Miscanthus* and some *Calamagrostis*). Summer also brings out the variegation and cross-banding of some miscanthus, intensifies the blue of the blue fescues (*Festuca*) and blue oat grass (*Helictotrichon sempervirens*), burnishes the bronze of various sedges (*Carex*), and reddens the blades of blood grass (*Imperata cylindrica*). Never without interest, and perfectly marvelous in some seasons, grass is a yearlong attraction in the landscape.

A flower-filled meadow may not have much to offer in winter, but what pleasure it brings when the snow is gone. As soon as the frost is out of the ground, up come the crocus, tulips, daffodils, and hyacinths. The display can dazzle us for two months, and that's only the prelude. Then the perennials join in—monochrome choruses, contrapuntal groups, and flashy soloists carry the show from spring through fall. And some might offer an encore of color and dried seed forms that retain their interest up to the edge of winter.

In addition to their unique visual appeal, both grasslands and meadows offer practical advantages. Both types of landscapes are inexpensive, easy to install, and quickly reach full effectiveness, and both are easy to maintain. How nice to have gardens that offer so much and demand so little.

Meadow of Daffodils

For a full six weeks, this meadow in Northampton, Massachusetts, is aglow with daffodils, the sunniest of spring flowers and among the most fragrant (Plate 48). They are used here in variety, and not the most ostentatious varieties, naturalized in the grasses among the trees. And naturalized they are, since daffodils, unlike most hybrid tulips and hyacinths, will happily increase their number year after year without attention.

How different the effect is from the usual approach, when daffodils (*Narcissus*) are arranged in beds and borders with geometric precision over the bare brown earth. Although we do love the art of pure geometry, a geometric planting of spring bulbs bores us to complete disinterest—we are unlikely to notice such a planting at all.

Of course, you might wonder about the impact of this garden after the flowers have faded. Then it is the gently sloping hill of grass and forested backdrop that define the landscape, creating a quieter picture with more emphasis on form than on color. Some may so miss the flowery spring display, however, that they may not be able to appreciate the more reserved effect that follows. The scene may be too minimalist for their tastes, maybe even too austere. For these people, some embellishments are in order. More

Plate 48. Meadow of daffodils, Northampton, Massachusetts.

111

color is what they need—a symphony of color in several movements—color in the summer, color in the fall, even color in the winter. One can easily modify this grassy meadow to provide just that.

Daffodil bulbs can be planted quite deeply, 9 to 10 in (23 to 25 cm) for the larger varieties (even deeper in colder climates where dormancy must be enforced until spring has come to stay). Since many annuals and perennials are shallow-rooted, this gives you the opportunity to plant over the bulbs. Choosing varieties with care will bring wave after wave of color throughout summer and fall, and even into winter if plants are selected that have ornamental seed heads, fruits, or evergreen foliage.

So this landscape can be customized to suit your taste: an extravaganza of blossoms from spring through fall, or a calmer, more subdued effect following the curtain-opening spectacular. If you are uncertain as to which persuasion to follow, opt for annuals to carry on the show, a plan that will allow you to thoroughly rework the design with little expense or labor every year.

Grassy Meadow with Birch

A grassy meadow, an isolated clump of birch, a forest backdrop—a simple, open composition, but, oh, so inviting. How pleasant it would be to stroll through the auburn grasses, to run your hand over the ivorine trunks of the birch, and to explore the cool shade of the forest.

The place is Crawford Notch State Park in the White Moun-

tains of New Hampshire (Plate 49); but with minor variations, such meadows can be found throughout much of the temperate zone. Autumn is the season, early autumn, and the grasses have already taken on their tawny hue. The paper birch (*Betula papyrifera*) is still in the process of a change of dress, showing as much green as yellow. Later, when the tree is stripped bare of foliage by winter, the graceful trunks stand out even more against the dark green conifers in the background.

When the grass renews itself in the spring, the birch and other deciduous trees put on a pointillistic display of translucent yellow-green. Even the more restrained conifers can't help but display a bit of enthusiasm with a show of new candles, standing out lighter and brighter against the old growth. When the landscape mellows into summer, the scene takes on more conservative tones of green and blue-green. Still, the white trunks of the birch provide contrast and line to the composition, as the entire landscape prepares itself for autumn once again.

Although the composition is strikingly simple, several features add variety and interest. The juxtaposition of deciduous and coniferous elements, particularly the birch and eastern white pine (*Pinus strobus*), plays an important role. The staggered background suggests a path leading into the forest—far more interesting than a uniform tree and shrub border. Of course, the sea of grass in the foreground is the central component of the design, an undulating carpet alive to the wind's whim, varying with sun and shade, and highly responsive to the change of seasons.

This is a robust composition; many alternative plants can be

Plate 49. Meadow and birch at Crawford Notch State Park in New Hampshire's White Mountains.

chosen with little change in the overall effect. Other white-barked birches could be used, such as the European white birch (*Betula pendula*), or the less graceful Asian white birch (*B. platyphylla*). Aspen (*Populus tremuloides*) has a place in colder climates; maybe *Stewartia* can be used in warmer ones. Many pines will supply the texture and color of the eastern white pine, though not the shape—it is that distinctive. Fir (*Abies*) or spruce (*Picea*) might work as well, but the result will be more formal. So many different meadow, prairie, and dryland grasses can be used that only your personal taste and climate can decide which is best. Any variation you choose should honor the subtle beauty of this landscape and uphold its gentle character.

A Mountain Meadow Near Timberline

Blue Lake—elevation 11,320 ft (3,450 m), nestled in a cirque between the summits of Pawnee Peak, Mount Toll, Paiute Peak, and Mount Audubon in the heart of Colorado's Rocky Mountains—is one of the most popular destinations in the Indian Peaks Wilderness Area. For those attuned to the pleasures to be found along the way, the lake is only the last reward of many offered by the trail to the top.

In mid- to late-summer, when most of the snow has finally left, the highcountry along the trail erupts in color. Flowers bloom wherever there is a patch of soil; they carpet hills, garland the banks of streams, and climb the flanks of mountains. The most lavish display is in the moisture-laden meadows (Plate 50). Here, violet-blue

Erigeron is found in broad sweeps contrasted with yellow *Arnica* and white *Achillea*, all this set against a backdrop of massive peaks. There is so much to enjoy that hikers who intended to go on to Blue Lake often are captured by the beauty of these meadows and spend the entire day here.

The surroundings add a great deal to the scene, to be sure, but a flower display of this kind would brighten any meadow, to the delight of those who walk its paths. What's more, such an effect, as stunning as it is, is both easy to realize and easy to maintain. The effect can be had from zone 2 through zone 8, in lands blessed with abundant moisture and in lands cursed by extended drought.

The window for the display seen here spans about a month, from mid-July to mid-August, but a bit of planning can easily extend the show from early spring to mid-fall, at least in climates and altitudes more moderate than those near Blue Lake. *Erigeron* provides the main theme here, but you can use *Aster*, both spring-blooming species and fall-blooming species, as well. You might change the color scheme during the season, making red or white the dominant hue with *Chrysanthemum*, *Pyrethrum*, or *Echinacea*. For a yellow display over a long period beginning in summer, there is no better choice than tickseed (*Coreopsis*) or brown-eyed Susan (*Rudbeckia fulgida*). Other plants for accent and contrast are too numerous to mention, but some of our favorites include yarrow (*Achillea*), red valerian or Jupiter's beard (*Centranthus*), *Salvia*, and *Veronica*.

In many temperate climates, beginning the show in early spring will require enlisting bulb plants: *Allium*, *Crocus*, daffodils (*Narcis-*

Plate 50. Mountain meadow near Blue Lake, Indian Peaks Wilderness Area, Colorado.

sus), *Hyacinthus* species, snowdrop (*Galanthus*), and tulip (*Tulipa*) species. The effect can be enjoyed from early March to June, and from zones 3 through 7, even longer in more moderate climates where other bulbs can be used. Fall bulbs, like autumn-flowering crocus, could extend the season to the leading edge of winter. Then only the falling snow would bring the curtain down on the flower show, but maybe by that time the eye will need a bit of a rest.

Of course, the appeal of the Blue Lake meadow goes well beyond just the flower display. The lay of the land, the trees and mountains in the background, and the pale granite boulders in the field all contribute to the effectiveness of this landscape. Unfortu-

nately, most garden interpretations of this design will have to do without the mountains. But a backdrop of evergreen trees might be practical, say pine (*Pinus*), fir (*Abies*), or spruce (*Picea*). To mirror this example from nature, the trees should not be large—semi-dwarf cultivars will best capture the stunting influence of the high-country. Boulders can be set in place in a planned pattern of seeming randomness, and the land can be contoured beforehand into gently rolling hills. You will still have to hike the trail to Blue Lake to get the full effect, but maybe the need to do so will be diminished a bit.

Chapter 5
WATER FEATURES

WATER in the landscape—the attraction is irresistible. We hike miles to see a waterfall, postpone lunch until we can find a spot near streamside, take our rest beside a lake. The lake need not be the size of Lake Tanganyika to make the trip worthwhile, and a waterfall need not rival that at Niagara to be memorable. Give it the right setting and even a small water feature will work its magic on you. Fallen leaves riding a stream, ripples on a lake putting on a light show, a cascades dancing about a rockfall— it's more than engaging, it's hypnotic.

Water features are also the focus of many of our favorite cultivated landscapes. Water in the garden—it reflects and enhances every mood that a landscape can evoke, from the most tranquil to the most animated, from utter calm to on-the-edge excitement. Gaze out over a pond, the water barely moving, reflecting the beauty of the surroundings in soft focus, the grasses by the shore nodding to their image with every breeze—pure serenity. What better invitation is there to relax and linger awhile? On the other hand, even a small stream rushing to the brink of even a modest

waterfall will set the pulse rate up a few notches. And on a hot day, one has to fight the urge to physically join the water in play, to soak some body part, or even to take the plunge altogether in the altogether.

Including water in the garden has practical benefits as well. A water feature primes the air and soil around it with the moisture needed to grow some very special plants; sedges, grasses, iris of many kinds, primulas, rodgersias, lotus, water lilies, and many others are right at home in such an environment. Other plants, such as the flowering cherries, dogwoods, and azaleas, prefer not to get their feet wet, yet seem especially designed for display next to water. It is as though their beauty is too great to be embraced by direct viewing alone—you also have to see their reflections in order to appreciate them fully.

Besides the psychological effect and its aesthetic contribution, and besides its horticultural advantages, using water in the garden can serve other purposes. A body of water is an excellent groundcover. You don't have to mow it, fertilize it, or thatch it, and you need not water it, except to replace what has evaporated. This is not to say that a water feature is entirely carefree, but surely it requires far less care than an equal area of bluegrass lawn. And in any size, it is far less boring.

We never tire of searching for water features, both along wilderness trails and in cultivated gardens. Over the years we have been fortunate in finding some extraordinary examples, some at planned destinations and some by chance. The hunt took us to some fairly exotic places, but others we found close to home. We begin with two superb examples in the Brooklyn Botanic Garden in New York.

GROTTO AND SLAB FALLS

Surrounded by big-city traffic and big-city crowds, New York's Brooklyn Botanic Garden is an oasis of serenity in a desert of glass, steel, and concrete. Every section of the garden provides some relief from the frantic pace, but none more so than the Japanese Hill-and-Pond Garden. The grand lake, with its red torii, its wisteria-draped viewing pavilion, its iris-studded shores, and its weeping flowering cherries on the bank, is surely the most famous attraction. It is much too large for a private garden, and much of its effect depends on its size. However, at the far end of the lake, across from the viewing platform, are two small water features of extraordinary beauty.

Stone Grotto

Tucked into a hillside in the Brooklyn Botanic Garden is a remarkable stone grotto (Plate 51). Several shallow caves work their way back into the hill, their shadowed interiors lending a bit of mystery to the scene. From the upper rim of one of the caves, slender cords of water fall into the shallow pool below, causing barely a ripple on the tranquil surface of the water or on the tranquil spirit of the scene.

A white *Wisteria* meanders across the rock, its sinuous branches and delicate white blossoms forming the perfect complement to the rugged, angular, dark stone walls that define the grotto. A Japanese maple (*Acer palmatum*), just out of view to the left, lends its grace and beauty to the composition. Protruding into the pool is a small peninsula, bare except for a few boulders, gravel, and a clump of yellow flag iris (*Iris pseudacorus*). Notice the controlled use of plants: few species carefully placed and meticulously maintained, without a scene-stealer in the show. The grotto is a model of harmony and restraint.

How can one construct a grotto such as this? With plastic pond liners and efficient water pumps, the pool and trickle falls present no problems. The stonework, however, requires some thought. Stones can be brought to the site, stacked, and held in place by mortar or steel rods set into drilled holes. Another solution would be to use cast stone, concrete poured and sculpted in place. There

Plate 51. Stone grotto, Brooklyn Botanic Garden, Brooklyn, New York.

is also the possibility of combining both methods of construction.

The plant material in this example is suitable for zones 5 through 7. Substitute clematis for the wisteria and Siberian maple (*Acer ginnala*) for the Japanese maple, and the design becomes suitable for zones 3 through 6.

Slab Falls

As though the grotto were not enough of a treat, 50 ft (15 m) or so uphill from the grotto is another treat: a small waterfall of simple elegance (Plate 52). Few visitors take the trouble to see it, and the few that do seldom stay long enough to give it its due. Too bad, because this feature, in spite of its modest size, is a gem. And it is just its limited size—a few feet wide and a few feet high—and its limited flow of water that make it so suitable for interpretation in a private garden.

What gives the water its play is a thin slab of rock, horizontally placed to define the lip of the falls. The overhang is deep enough to cast a shadow on the supporting wall, the black background a perfect foil for the macramé of glistening strands of water. A small stream feeds the falls and gently tumbles into a small pond.

The plants surrounding the falls are in keeping with its unassuming naturalism; there are no scene-stealers and all growth is controlled. Harmony characterizes the design of this little garden, and harmony is what it communicates.

Plate 52. Slab falls, Brooklyn Botanic Garden, Brooklyn, New York.

Azalea and Cascades

A small stream choreographed over a series of stone steps, and an azalea trained to overhang the water—these are the components of an exquisite arrangement, simple enough to be taken in at a glance, special enough to be long-remembered (Plate 53). The design has a distinctly oriental aura, and in fact it is part of the Japanese garden in the Stanley Park in Westfield, Massachusetts. But this does not mean that the feature would be out of place in other kinds of gardens, for its straightforward beauty transcends any regionalism.

We came upon this scene in early spring. The deciduous azalea (*Rhododendron*), thinned and pruned to accentuate its graceful line, was at peak bloom. So striking was the effect that it took us awhile before we could see and appreciate the other elements of the design. The dark rock and the action of the water is what sets the stage for the flower show, and these are the elements that will carry the design through the many months when the azalea is not in bloom—an important consideration, since that amounts to about eleven months out of the year.

Fortunately, many deciduous azaleas, both hybrids and species, are not only stunning in flower, but are also elegant in leaf and put on a show of autumn color that rivals that of their spring display. In addition, many selections will present a graceful tracery of bare branches against the falls in winter, an effect often heightened by a coating of snow or a glistening coat of ice.

Unfortunately, not every region is azalea-land, and we know of no substitute that will serve quite as well. However, where soil and climate rule out the use of azaleas, we might consider one of the smaller flowering plums (*Prunus*), or a dwarf crabapple (*Malus*). Both are easily pruned to shape and offer a superb spring show of flowers. *Fothergilla* is a possibility, but it will give a different effect in flower; no one will complain about its autumn show.

Companion plants for groundcover or for flowers should be kept to a minimum; elegant simplicity is the hallmark of this design and is what makes it so effective. Restraint in embellishing this design will keep its maintenance to a minimum, and it will assure that the pleasure derived from it is maximum.

Plate 53. Azalea and cascades, Stanley Park, Westfield, Massachusetts.

A Woodland Stream in Autumn

Water features are the main attraction in Tannery Falls State Park in Massachusetts. The area boasts streams, rivers, cascades, and several magnificent waterfalls. Tannery Falls itself is the finest of these, but it is far too large for any garden other than nature's own.

Walking along the paths near the base of the falls, however, we came across an unnamed stream of modest proportions, small enough to adapt to a garden setting without altering its scale. Here the leisurely flow presents water in its most serene mood, and the gentle forest enhances the tranquility. Even in autumn, as seen in our photograph (Plate 54), the modulation of color is more subtle than boisterous, and the overall effect remains restful. We have also seen this landscape after a snowstorm in early November, when the stream was still free of ice. At that time, under a low and feeble sun, the scene was a study in black and white: the linear pattern of the trees etched against the snow, and the steely blue-black ribbon of water barely flowing.

The scene is strikingly different in the spring and summer, but no less lovely. In spring, translucent lime-green leaves catch the light like stained glass. The water picks up this color and enlivens it still more, and the stream itself becomes almost rambunctious at the prodding of the spring rains and melted snow. During the summer months, although the colors are more reserved, the entire forest assumes a greater presence, while the stream thins to a lesser role.

This is one of the most appealing qualities of this landscape, the way it interacts with the seasons, and a cultivated version of it is bound to give the same rewards. Again we want to emphasize that streams like this are now easy to construct in your own backyard. A plastic pool liner will make the stream bed watertight. Gravel along the bottom and boulders along the banks will hide the plastic. Submersible electrical pumps will circulate the water for mere pennies a day.

Selecting trees for a streamside forest presents all sorts of possibilities. Birches, such as paper birch (*Betula papyrifera*) and European white birch (*B. pendula*), are near the top of the list for their elegance, their white bark, and their tawny golden fall color. Japanese and fullmoon maples (*Acer palmatum* and *A. japonicum*), hedge maple (*A. campestre*), Oregon vine maple (*A. circinatum*), Shantung maple (*A. truncatum*), Siberian maple (*A. ginnala*), and others would make a nice contribution all year long. *Stewartia* and mountain ash (*Sorbus*) would also fit nicely, but these and the maples might steal the scene in autumn.

Shrubs for the understory might include *Rhododendron, Viburnum*, mountain laurel (*Kalmia*), Japanese andromeda (*Pieris japonica*), and many others. Nor is there much of a restriction on the choice of groundcovers and perennials. So there is an opportunity to mix and match the forest elements, but take care not to obscure the main component of the model: the meandering stream that ties this landscape together. The only risk is overdoing it, letting the details distract from the overall picture and diluting the gentle impact that the original scene evokes.

Plate 54. Stream in autumn, Tannery Falls State Park, Massachusetts.

A Rock-Locked, Mighty-Mite of a Waterfall

Another one of the many small wonders to be found in Tannery Falls State Park in Massachusetts lies a bit off the trail that leads to the great falls for which the park is named. It's a rock-locked, mighty-mite of a waterfall, a waist-high, pint-size dynamo (Plate 55). Caught in the convolutions of the black stone, it expresses its displeasure with being contained by thrashing itself into white foam—pure energy, pure excitement. Squint away the background and the size of the falls is impossible to estimate; it could be 15 ft (4.5 m) tall or 1 ft (0.3 m) tall, and either way it would communicate the same feeling of boundless energy barely contained.

Of course, in its 3-ft (0.9-m) size or a smaller version, the effect could be easily diluted by not giving it the room it needs to flex its muscles. Avoid crowding it with other features; avoid placing large plants next to it that would steal its thunder; and avoid close proximity to buildings. Give this little dynamo its due space, stand back, and tap the energy that it generates.

To get the kind of action needed, a considerable amount of water has to be moved. A trickle or two won't do; enough has to be lifted and directed so as to give it a head of foam. Otherwise, much of the effect will be lost. But this is not a large feature, and compared to many waterfalls that are seen in garden settings, the demands are not that extravagant. Besides, how can you weigh the worth of something this energizing and this beautiful in pennies per kilowatt?

Plate 55. A rock-locked, mighty-mite waterfall in Tannery Falls State Park, Massachusetts.

Waterfall—Pure and Simple

In the middle of the nineteenth century, after amassing a fortune in real estate and the cutlery business, the English expatriate Henry Shaw decided to build a grand public garden on his estate in St. Louis, Missouri. And grand it became under the efforts of some of the best landscape architects and most renowned botanists of the time. The project expanded to nearly 80 acres, and became the Missouri Botanical Garden, the first public garden in the United States. One of its most popular attractions, the Japanese garden, offers a variety of water features: a lake, a stream, and a superb waterfall (Plate 56).

The waterfall is only about 4 ft (1.2 m) tall, but its simple design gives it a monumentality that hides its dimensions. It could be half its true size or twice its true size—only the plants that surround it allow us to make an estimate. A thin sheet of water slips over a ledge perched between the peaks of two large black boulders. The falling water forms a translucent curtain, half of which drops directly into the basin below, while the other half is folded to the left by a smaller pair of boulders. Framing the waterfall is a canyon, the walls of which are planted with evergreen and deciduous shrubs, meticulously pruned but convincingly natural. Our photograph, taken in early fall, hints at the striking contrast that will develop between the red leaves of a Japanese maple (*Acer palmatum*) and the green of the surrounding plants.

A waterfall of this size is certainly suitable for a private garden or a small public garden. St. Louis is in zone 6, but the plants used here would be happy enough in zones 5 or 7, and the design could

Plate 56. Waterfall at the Missouri Botanical Garden, St. Louis, Missouri.

127

easily be pushed into zone 3 by substituting a Siberian maple (*Acer ginnala*) for the Japanese maple. Finding suitable rock and setting it in place is the greatest difficulty. Piecing stones together to get the dimensions needed will not give the monumentality of the original, and a single stone of the right size and shape might be hard to find. The stone we see has no complicated features, however, and it would be easy to make a reasonable likeness in cement. And any reasonable likeness, as long as the strong form of the original is honored, should give a design that will be the garden's center of interest.

Caribbean Paradise

If the waterfall shown in Plate 57 evokes images of lush tropical forests, pristine beaches, and sultry offshore breezes, you are not being misled. The scene in the photo is from Carinosa Gardens on the island of Jamaica. The intense dappled sunlight, the exuberant plant growth, and the calypso rhythm of the water all play to the image—this is the tropics.

The scene you see is the product of a collaboration, a hybrid construction where natural elements were modified and adorned by people with an eye for found beauty and the respect for nature required to showcase it. The basic structure of the falls was in place long before Jamaica appeared on any map. The stone framework divides and rejoins the falling stream into a complex pattern of interacting parts—liquid macramé on a grand scale. The surrounding forest was cleared and refurbished with plants that are mostly native to the island, although with all the inter-island and mainland-to-island travel by humans and other creatures, it is often impossible to track down the origins of the plants. Indigenous or not, it all fits together perfectly, and the entire landscape seems perfectly natural.

The falls is about 10 ft (3 m) tall, but you can't be blamed if you underestimate its height by comparing it to the white blossoms overhanging the stream. Those are the flowers of datura (*Datura* or *Brugmansia*), a shrub that produces magnificent silken-white deliciously fragrant trumpets nine months a year; the size of the blossoms is a full 10 in (25 cm) from end to end. An ornamental banana (*Musa*) displays its huge leaves besides the falls; other tropicals in flower add color to the base of the falls. We still remember the exotic fragrances that perfume the site. It's paradise, or at least as close to it as most of us will ever get.

Can mere mortals who do not live in the tropics have an approximation of this garden? Absolutely! The exotic effect of the garden is due mostly to the plants that frame it; the waterfall itself would be a prized feature in any zone. Although many of the plants in Carinosa Gardens would take such umbrage at the mere mention of frost that they would leave this world altogether, many possible stand-ins made of far sturdier stuff will carry the design into zone 4. The flowering shrubs could be azalea (*Rhododendron*), or *Weigela* for an even longer period of bloom. In zone 6, *Fuchsia* offers so much variety that little else is needed to complete the foreground. Maybe dwarf roses (*Rosa*) with small five-petaled blossoms would work. Even a dwarf mockorange (*Philadelphus*) might be

Plate 57. Waterfall in a Caribbean paradise, Carinosa Gardens, Jamaica.

considered, but here the choice is between white and white—although the scent would add the perfect touch.

A substitute for the main plant in the picture, the datura, presents a greater problem. We can think of none that is completely satisfactory, at least none that will give the desired effect for months and remain in the ground year-round. Unfortunately, the datura is a main feature in this landscape and does much to define its character. Of course, if you are willing to make a concession or two, and you have the facilities to house the plant over winter, then you can have your datura in a pot, the pot brought out into the garden during milder weather and brought indoors for the remaining time. With such devotion and care you could also use a potted orchid tree (*Bauhinia*).

But if it's in-the-ground or not-at-all, the Darwinian do-or-die approach, you could consider a late-blooming, long-flowering, small cultivar of the kousa dogwood (*Cornus kousa*) planted to the side, where its roots will not soak in the water, and thinned and pruned to a few branches overhanging the base of the falls. A zone 4 hardy hibiscus, *Hibiscus syriacus*, can be treated in the same way, but its growth is even more intractable than that of kousa dogwood. Other less convincing possibilities include a large azalea (*Rhododendron*), or a small shrubby crabapple (*Malus*) or plum or cherry (*Prunus*), but these have only a brief flowering period in early to mid-spring.

Of course, the choice of plants will determine how tropical the garden appears. How much of the tropics should be evoked is a question that the designer will have to decide: more for the fan of pink polyester flamingos strutting their stuff in a Minnesota snowstorm, less for those of the grow-native persuasion. Either way you design it, it should bring a bit of paradise to your doorstep.

Waterfall in a Jungle Under Glass

The air is moist and warm, and a gentle breeze carries the scent of exotic blossoms. Figs and frangipani, palms and pandanus, and all sorts of other strange and wondrous trees vie for their share of sunlight. Bromeliads, orchids, philodendrons, and ferns festoon the branches. Gingers, begonias, alocasias, and anthuriums crowd the understory. No, this is not the Amazon Jungle or a South Sea Island—this is St. Louis, Missouri, and it is a jungle under glass. This tropical paradise is encapsulated beneath the great geodesic dome of the Missouri Botanical Garden's Climatron (Plate 58).

A maze of paths leads into the heart of this jungle. One trail passes under a pandanus tree, perched on its stilt legs like a crane, its winglike fronds spreading above you. Framed by the fronds and set deep into a canyon, its source hidden by a thicket of plants, a waterfall drops 6 ft (1.8 m) or so into a basin. The mist generated by the falls bathes the banks and walls of the canyon, placing the entire scene in soft focus. Enough light filters through to weave the shadows of the plants on the water, and the motion of the water gives motion to the shadows, causing them to squirm and jiggle like living creatures. It's all quite magical, quite exotic. It may not be the tropics, but it satisfies our most romantic, idealized notion of what the tropics is like.

Plate 58. Waterfall in a jungle under glass at the Missouri Botanical Garden, St. Louis, Missouri.

Where do you place such a feature if you don't own a Climatron? Reduce the height a bit and it can be tucked into almost any garden. It should be in some corner, recessed into the contours of the land, in order to capture the mysterious mood of the original. The effect will be lost if it is placed in too conspicuous a site.

As for the plants, there are a great many from which to choose. To capture the tropical appearance of this example in an outdoor setting, the smaller rodgersias, hostas, ferns, sedges, and grasses can be used. *Iris* and *Primula* can be used in moderation to provide a spot of color. But what of the pandanus? That requires a greater compromise. Not similar, but thoroughly appropriate, a Japanese maple (*Acer palmatum*), a fullmoon maple (*A. japonicum*), or its stand-in, an Oregon vine maple (*A. circinatum*), nearly suggest the tropics and are far more graceful than pandanus.

So dense are the plants and so active is the water that we were not able to determine whether the canyon and the structure supporting the falls is constructed of natural stone, concrete, or a combination of these. Either approach will work, but concrete might be the least expensive and most convenient alternative for most situations. Even an approximation will transport us to the tropics. Fix me a mai-tai, please.

Lordvale Falls

A magnificent waterfall distinguishes the grounds of the Lordvale Condominiums in Grafton, Massachusetts, and it is the waterfall that deserves a grandiose name like Lordvale, not the ordinary

complex of buildings. The falls is a mere 9 ft (2.7 m) tall, but its monumental presence commands all its surroundings (Plate 59). Because of the skillful selection and placement of plants around it, it is seamlessly integrated into the rest of the landscape.

The framework of the falls is made of natural granitic stone, huge slabs stood on end and abutted lengthwise to give the water an almost clear descent to the base. The water tumbles onto a shallow stream bed and there spreads out across flat shards of the same stone. It's an imposing structure, one of stark beauty and power.

The nearly formal architectural lines of the waterfall are softened by a planting of shrubs: red-leaved barberries (*Berberis*) stand out among mugo pines (*Pinus mugo*), azaleas (*Rhododendron*), and others. There are no showoffs in the planting, no competing architectural elements, no scene-stealing perennials to upstage the play of the magnificent waterfall. And so the scene seems harmonious, even tranquil, in spite of the power of the design and the action of the water.

The plants used in the design are widely available and widely adaptable in zones 4 through 7. Other choices can easily be found to accommodate other zones. Honoring the design only requires restraint in the number of species used and in their showiness. Mainly, the plants need to be neat by nature or by culture.

The framework of the falls, on the other hand, even in a smaller version, requires large stones, and such stones are not easy to find and not easy to move. Using smaller stones and piecing them together would compromise the impact of the design, but cast stone might work. Finishing the design with shards of real stone at the

Plate 59. Lordvale Falls, Grafton, Massachusetts.

base of the falls is easy enough, but the cast stone would have to be matched carefully in color and texture. Although the construction of this feature requires more thought and expense than some others described here, it is impressive enough to justify the additional cost and effort.

Although the integrity of the design allows you to imagine the falls leaping over the rim 50 ft (15 m) above your head, a version no taller than 5 ft (1.5 m) would also be impressive; and at that height such a falls could grace almost any garden. Nevertheless, the shear monumentality of the design argues for its use on some public grounds or at least on a large lot far from any building. Give it its space, and Lordvale Falls will reign supreme over its domain.

Golden Gate Waterfall

Golden Gate Park in San Francisco, California, is so popular that it is hard to see the forest for the people. They come to picnic, to jog, to see and be seen. Some even come to enjoy the beautifully planned gardens and the great plant collections—not easy to do when a mob surrounds you on all sides. But, with a bit of walking, it is possible to find more isolated sections of the park where one can be alone with only a few dozen other visitors. In such a place is a remarkable waterfall (Plate 60), one so large, so imposing, that you would think it would attract throngs. Fortunately, it seldom does.

The stone framework of the falls towers overhead, perhaps to 15 ft (4.5 m) or more, and extends twice that in width. The volume and action of the water are as impressive as the structure, with sev-eral major and minor flows interacting in a tangle of complex patterns. The stone walls taper inward toward each other and seem to magnify the force of the falls by focusing the flow. The water collects in a good-size pool, from which it is shunted away beneath a walk of cast-stone slabs of irregular shape, precisely pieced together to create an effect much like that created by nature a continent away at the top of Cadillac Mountain in Maine's Acadia National Park (see Plate 13 in Chapter 2). Large boulders are grouped at the base of the falls, where they direct the flow and provide the setting for the few plants in the composition. Dominating the arrangement at the water's edge is *Gunnera manicata*, growing in clumps as tall as a human and with leaf blades as large as an African elephant's ear. The boldness of the plant fits the boldness of the overall design perfectly.

The first impression on seeing this magnificent waterfall is that it is too bold, too audacious, and certainly too grand in scale to be realized on anything less than the grounds of a public park. Seen in a photograph, however, isolated and abstracted from its surroundings, with no indication of its size except that revealed by the *Gunnera*, one can easily imagine that the falls is several times greater than its actual size or that it is much less than its actual size. It has a geometric integrity that allows a variety of size interpretations without violating the overall design—without trivializing it and without exaggerating it—and this is what makes it such an apt model for all sorts of garden situations, where its boldness and strength can serve as the central feature.

As for the construction, it is unlikely that real stone of the

Plate 60. Waterfall at Golden Gate Park, San Francisco, California.

appropriate size and shape can be found to fit the design, although that is a possibility. A more likely approach is to follow the lead of the model itself, which is made entirely of cast stone and concrete, convincingly colored and modeled to look like real stone.

Plant options for climates colder than that required by *Gunnera* (zone 7) include *Rodgersia*, *Ligularia*, umbrella plant (*Peltiphyllum peltatum*), Japanese butterbur (*Petasites japonicus*), and ornamental rhubarb (*Rheum*), all of which are hardy to zone 4. Among the many others that can be used to complement these are rush (*Scirpus*), Japanese silver grass (*Miscanthus sinensis*), and *Iris*. Once again, restraint in the use of plants serves this design best and is the recipe for carefree enjoyment of this kind of feature season after season.

Cascades: A Rough and Tumble Play of Water

A gently meandering stream never fails to evoke a sense of calm and relaxation. But the stream along Falling Waters Trail in Franconia Notch State Park, New Hampshire, does not meander gently (Plate 61). It dashes to its destination through an obstacle course of rock ledges set counter to its movement. Here, the theme is action, frenetic action that animates the entire scene. No leisurely waltz this; it's a stop-and-start, twist-and-turn tango, and no ballroom dance can match the energy of its syncopated rhythm.

To get such an effect to such a degree requires a substantial flow of water, a flow on a scale unlikely to be practical in most cultivated landscapes. So downscaling is in order, although downscaling will lessen the effect somewhat. But maybe the original is so frenetic that it would be tiring to see it over and over again. Toning it down a bit might in fact make the design more suitable for gardens, not less. Even a smaller version will be the main attraction if given the chance, and all that is needed to give it a chance is to give it enough room. Avoid overplanting the banks and background; avoid plants that are too large or overly flamboyant. Give it space and you will give it its due. In return, you capture the spirit of the spring runoff collecting in a mountain stream—you capture the energy.

For those who find this cascades too exciting, too rambunctious, our next example might be more suitable.

Plate 61. Rough and tumble cascades along Falling Water Trail, Franconia Notch State Park, New Hampshire.

Cascades: Montreal Botanical Garden

A cascades of a very different mood than the one just visited is found in Canada's Montreal Botanical Garden (Plate 62). The previous example was wild in location and wild in spirit. This one is tame, designed for a garden setting and reserved in its action. The flow is never constrained, never directed against itself in crosscurrents, never thrashed to white foam by a precipitous drop or an obstructing boulder. Instead, it proceeds downhill, step-by-step in a leisurely fashion, making its way over a descending sequence of flat slabs of stone, each step no more than 12 in (30 cm) higher than the next. The course of the cascades is laid out in a series of gentle curves, a perfect setting for all sorts of plants that look good and grow well next to water.

Grasses play a major role in this design, and no group of plants is better suited for the purpose. Japanese silver grass (*Miscanthus sinensis*) is a superb choice and is represented by several cultivars. One could also use clumps of goose-necked loosestrife (*Lysimachia clethroides*) or brown-eyed loosestrife (*L. punctata*); Japanese, Louisiana, yellow flag, or any one of many types of *Iris*; *Acorus calamus* or *A. gramineus* in some variegated form; rushes like *Scirpus tabernaemontana* 'Zebrinus'; or horsetail (*Equisetum*). A variety of different species of ferns could also be used. Many of the typical hardy water-lovers, such as butterbur (*Petasites*), *Rodgersia*, *Ligularia*, and umbrella plant (*Peltiphyllum*), might be too coarse or too bold for this application, however.

A cascades such as this, with wide shallow steps, is relatively easy to construct. The individual stones that make up the steps have little character and need no more than they have. Such stone is fairly inexpensive, is easily moved, and is easily set in place. Although the stream is several feet (a meter or so) wide, it is slow moving and shallow, so the volume of water moved is moderate. This makes a scaled-down version practical even for a private garden. The planting should not overwhelm the principal attraction: the meandering stream, sliding from level to level across the shelves of rock. This is an unassuming water feature, quietly beautiful, and richly rewarding. Any interpretation of it should retain this essential character.

Plate 62. Gentle cascades, Montreal Botanical Garden, Montreal, Canada.

Lost Man Lake

Smuggler's Notch in northwestern Vermont is one of many magnificent canyons in the Green Mountains. And green those mountains are, green with thick groves of mixed hardwoods and conifers. Forests this dense, this heavy with leaves, reflect the abundance of moisture lavished on the region—it's on the verge of being a rain forest.

It was through a drizzling rain that we hiked up Smuggler's Notch to Lost Man Lake. Thoroughly wet and thoroughly miserable, we did not see the lake until we were within a few paces of it. There, in the mist, the distant shore blended imperceptibly into the gray sky, and the forest flanking it on either side was barely visible. Within a few feet of the near shore, a small island, perhaps 15 ft (4.5 m) across its largest dimension, seemed to float on the mist (Plate 63). A few dwarfed conifers had made the island their home. Not even Monet could have captured this picture. We soon forgot the dampness and cold, and gave thanks to the mist and rain for presenting this scene to us in this way. Now we were the lost men, lost in the magic of this place.

We have not been back to this lake, and we never have seen it in sunlight, but surely it must be a wonder then, too: the sparkling water playing about the small island and reflecting its dwarfed trees. And what it must be like in early winter, the water still unfrozen and the conifers dusted with snow or glistening with ice. Surely, it is a joy in every season. For us, in search of garden themes, the island was a true prize, small enough to adorn a lake of modest size in a cultivated garden.

Since many genetically dwarf firs (*Abies*), spruces (*Picea*), hemlocks (*Tsuga*), and pines (*Pinus*) are available to choose from, planting such an island is easy enough. Companion plants can be selected from water-tolerant dwarf hollies (*Ilex*), azaleas (*Rhododendron*), or shrubby dogwoods (*Cornus*). Small grasses and flowering perennials in moderation can be used to complete the picture. The goal here is not to wash the island in color, not to obscure its overall design, but to provide a bit of color here and there to mark the passing of the seasons. The overall plan is what makes the impression, and capturing that is the challenge.

Plate 63. Lost Man Lake, Smuggler's Notch, Green Mountain State Park, Vermont.

Lake in a Sunken Garden

An abandoned limestone quarry is not the most likely place to find inspiration for a landscape design. One is even less likely to come upon a garden featuring a superb lake in such a place. But that is exactly the setting of the renowned Sunken Garden in Butchart Gardens in Victoria, British Columbia, Canada.

At the turn of the century, the quarry supplied the limestone for the Butchart family's cement business. When the quarry was depleted, Mrs. Butchart decided to turn it and its surroundings into a garden, to make something of lasting beauty out of what otherwise was destined to be something of monumental ugliness. Butchart Gardens is the legacy of her vision.

The gardens occupy about 50 acres and include a formal rose garden, an even more formal Italian garden, and a Japanese garden, all magnificently designed and meticulously maintained. Other sections of the gardens are best described as semi-formal. Well-manicured lawns set the stage for plantings of trees and shrubs. While not regimented by rank and file, these specimen plants were chosen for their unusual shapes and colors rather than their naturalness. Bright yellow conifers are juxtaposed against purple-foliaged deciduous trees; weeping trees are set against fastigiate selections; dwarfs are pitted against giants. The style blends old world graciousness with new world pizzazz. In places the planting and arrangement look anything but natural, although the beauty of the scene cannot be denied.

On our tour, our interest is in the garden within the quarry, where the style changes to one that is much more naturalistic. A stairway leads down the vine-draped wall to the bottom, and a short path takes you to the lake (Plate 64). Here the landscape looks like a piece of wilderness—a bit idealized, a bit romanticized, but wilderness nevertheless.

The lake is pear-shaped, the neck end narrow enough to serve as a model for a private garden on a lot of modest size. The bank is strongly contoured and in places rises steeply to nearly 6 ft (1.8 m) above the water. Moisture-loving perennials—some bold, some delicate—grow along the bank. Primulas contrast nicely with Japanese butterbur (*Petasites japonicus*); *Rodgersia*, *Iris*, ferns, and double marsh marigold (*Caltha palustris*) lend their diverse colors and textures to the scene. Azaleas (*Rhododendron*) are used in abundance. Japanese maples (*Acer palmatum*), flowering cherries (*Prunus*), crabapples (*Malus*), birch (*Betula*), willows (*Salix*), and other trees and shrubs give the appearance that the lake is surrounded by a forest, and they help to isolate this section from the less naturalistic features in the other parts of the garden. Photographed here in the spring, when the azaleas are at their peak and the garden is at its flowery best, this is very much a landscape to enjoy throughout the year, a landscape that offers a different treat in every season.

The plants that we see here are adapted to a wide range of climates, from the warmer parts of zone 4 to zone 7, but these limits can easily be pushed to include zones 3 and 8 by using more crabapples, shrub cherries, Siberian maple (*Acer ginnala*), and shrub dog-

Plate 64. Lake in the Sunken Garden at Butchart Gardens in Victoria, British Columbia, Canada.

woods (*Cornus*) and using fewer flowering cherries, azaleas, and Japanese maples. This design is strong enough to accommodate many variations and still retain its identity: a serene lake surrounded by an idealized forest. What more pleasant place to spend an afternoon.

A Wilderness Waterfall Urbanized

It's water features like the one we feature here (Plate 65) that draw city folk into the forest and lure flatlanders to climb mountains. But the residents of the Highline Apartments in Aurora, Colorado, need only step outside the building to experience this piece of nature. And the waterfall is only part of the landscape; also included is a meandering stream, some aspen, and a small grove of blue spruce (see also Plate 79).

One of the blue spruces (*Picea pungens*) is seen on the left of the photo; the branch of an aspen (*Populus tremuloides*) hangs over the stream on the right; and juniper (*Juniperus*) borders the scene at the bottom. The plants frame the scene perfectly and direct our attention to the waterfall and the stream. The water plays over a rock structure that is itself a piece of sculpture, complicated and asymmetrical, yet well-balanced and fascinating from all angles. The complexity of the rockwork is further reflected in the action of the water, dividing and rejoining as it falls to the base. There is even a side branch of the falls that forms a cascades, tumbling over several steps to the stream below. No matter how often we see this landscape, it continues to engage us. The design is so rich in interacting components that it cannot be fully appreciated in only a few visits, and there always seems to be some aspect of it that escaped our attention before.

Natural rock was used throughout the construction; there is no cast stone. The shapes of the boulders and the way they abut would be difficult to capture in cast stone unless the boulders were individually molded and then stacked. But this would require far more time, effort, and expense than bringing in natural rock, provided natural rock is locally available.

Availability is not a problem with the plants used here; they can be found in nurseries throughout zones 3 through 7. For those who feel that these plants are overused, or for those living in warmer climates, a great many alternatives are possible. The blue spruce can be replaced by a blue clone of atlas cedar (*Cedrus atlantica*) or white fir (*Abies concolor*). Any tree with an open structure and slender trunk and branches can be used in place of the aspen. Low-growing cultivars of yew (*Taxus*), *Euonymus*, grapeholly (*Mahonia*), true holly (*Ilex*), and *Pyracantha* are among the many evergreen groundcovers that can be substituted for the juniper. The particular plants used are not essential for the effect—the design is that strong. It's the water feature that has center stage, and nothing should compete with it—very little can.

Plate 65. Urban waterfall, Aurora, Colorado.

A small patch of forest in Crawford Notch State Park, New Hampshire.

Chapter 6

FOREST WALKS

*N*OWHERE do you feel so in touch with a landscape as when strolling through a forest. There the wonder and beauty surround you on all sides—even above in the weaving of leaves and branches against the sky, even at your feet in the tapestry of groundcovers. And no landscape provides such dramatic changes from season to season, at least in those climates where there are seasons.

If yours is not an estate of a dozen acres or more, however, the thought of a backyard forest might seem to be an oxymoronic pipe-dream. After all, a tree or two does not a forest make, and to grow a grove requires time, more than a lifetime if you are starting from acorns and want a mature grove of oaks. But not every tree is an oak, and the time needed to create the effect of a young forest in a garden of modest size is better measured in seasons than in years. Much depends on the appropriate choice of trees and shrubs.

Luckily, some of the most magnificent forest trees are fast growing and can add several feet (a meter or more) of growth per year. Even some of the conifers are capable of a yearly growth of more than 1 ft (0.3 m). So even young nursery stock will soon give you the feel of a forest, with trees large enough to stand under, large enough to provide some shade and protection from the wind, and large enough to be the most prominent and valued component of your landscape.

Besides privacy and yearlong beauty, what more does a garden forest offer? Gardens where trees are grown in clumps and groves, as they often grow in nature, are usually horticulturally sound. Trees such as birch, aspen, various maples, some oaks, sassafras, and many conifers look their best and grow their best under these conditions. Although some of these trees are short-lived and disease-prone, they tend to send up new growth from the roots, providing a constant source of renewal for those that are used up. A stand of trees with members of various ages creates an effect that is both natural and dynamic.

Another advantage of a garden forest is that it is fairly easy to maintain. Its informality forgives the occasional broken branch and the misplaced volunteer. You can even ignore a few weeds. All sorts of groundcovers are appropriate for the floor of a garden forest, so the area given over to grass can be kept to a minimum, and this too helps to keep the maintenance chores manageable.

Even a small garden forest quickly becomes a wildlife sanctuary. Birds and other critters are soon attracted to such a garden—after all, it's a place where they can find food and shelter. The authors' backyard forest in Boulder, Colorado, passes for the real thing among a whole menagerie of beasts that come to call, or call it home; birds of dozens of different species, squirrels, muskrats, rabbits, raccoons, skunks, and an occasional fox make our garden theirs. We have even had the "pleasure" of receiving a cougar for a brief visit—nothing like a visit from a cougar to keep you wide-eyed and alert in the garden. True, some of the uninvited visitors give us grief in measure far exceeding their size, but most are welcome and provide us with four seasons of pure pleasure. So we tolerate the nasties while encouraging the others, and together we enjoy a private bit of forest. It's a privilege; it's a treat. No other landscape brings more rewards.

We will tour forests of mixed hardwoods, coniferous forests, and forests combining evergreen and deciduous trees. But first we visit several forests in which trees of only one species dominate, trees of incomparable grace and beauty.

ALDER, BIRCH, AND ASPEN

White bark marked with black or brocaded in auburn, rust, or green lichens; limbs and twigs finely drawn and delicately set; slen-

der trunks closely spaced or growing in clumps to form stunning patterns of light and dark—all this sets forests of aspen, birch, or alder apart from others. No matter how densely planted, these forests always seem light and open, youthful and full of vitality.

In addition to their unique design attributes, these trees offer several horticultural advantages. They are fairly fast-growing and are easily propagated from seed. Collected specimens, particularly aspen, are readily available and inexpensive. Alder and aspen sucker at the roots, and so a grove continually renews itself, presenting a balance of old and young trees that is as naturalistic as it is beautiful.

On the other hand, these trees share some damnable faults. Short-lived by genetic design, their time in a planting is often curtailed by infections of rusts, molds, and bacteria, and they play host to all sorts of other plagues. If a creature chews, bores, burrows, or gnaws, these trees will be its target of choice. Be it beetle or beaver, deer or rabbit, the thin-skinned boles offer an irresistible nosh. We can only hope that plant breeders will someday develop disease- and insect-resistant cultivars and gain for themselves our everlasting gratitude.

Another fault has to be mentioned, but this is a fault of our species, not of the trees. The white bark—the ease with which one can pare into it and the hideous black scarring that results—make these the preferred trees to vandalize by jackknife-wielding jackasses. For this disease, we see no cure.

But, as that old song says, with all their faults, we love them still, these exquisite trees. We planted several clumps of aspen in our own garden; we should have known better. We spray them with dormant oil, with fungicides, with insecticides. We paint them with animal repellent and guard the trunks with cylinders of wire mesh. And we curse the trees, their diseases, and their predators— we do a lot of cursing. But we tolerate their faults, for these lovely trees make unique landscapes, and we know of no substitutes.

Alder in the Pacific Northwest

In the cool and misty climate of the Pacific Northwest, the red alder (*Alnus rubra*) is common enough to be considered a weed tree. But what a superb weed it is, slender-boled and elegant in form, often congregating in clumps, the individual stems gracefully splaying outward and then arching backward and upward. The bark is a patchwork quilt of the most subtle and satisfying patterns: patterns in brown-gray and white created by lichens and peeling layers of bark. Although red alder can reach a height of 90 ft (27 m), growing them in clumps or dense groves keeps them at 20 ft (6 m) or so.

On the Yurok Loop Trail in Redwood National Park, California, we came upon a small stand of red alder bordering the path (Plate 66). A simple wooden fence separated the path from the trees and brought a touch of the human hand to the scene, making this little piece of wilderness seem very much like a garden. See how the habit of the trees is influenced by the presence of the path. A little more sunlight, a little more water, and a little less root competition gives the trees near the edge of the path a growth advantage, and they stretch and bend over the path to get even more.

Plate 66. Alder along Yurok Loop Trail, Redwood National Park, California.

149

The effect is seen again in another section of the park, on the Redwood Creek Trail (Plate 67). Here the branches of the trees knit together above the path, creating a natural *allée* precise enough to have graced an eighteenth-century French garden. Yet the effect is as rustic as it is sophisticated, bold as it is graceful. This scene, too, is easy to picture as part of a cultivated garden, although the space required is much greater.

Creating such an effect in a landscape setting of human design requires some thought. Unfortunately, red alder has a restricted range of adaptability, and there aren't many trees that can offer the same graceful lines and extraordinary bark pattern. In zones 3 to 7, gray birch (*Betula populifolia*) might be a good choice; paper birch (*B. papyrifera*) or European white birch (*B. pendula*) are also possibilities. From zones 7 to 9, crapemyrtle (*Lagerstroemia indica*) might be considered. It often grows as a multi-stemmed tree, has superbly patterned bark, and offers nearly three months of exquisite summer bloom with panicles of white, pink, or purple—an advantage or disadvantage, depending on how you see it. Certainly, the effect would be different, but maybe just as pleasing. But it's with alder, birch, or aspen that the design will best be represented.

Plate 67. Alder along Redwood Creek Trail, Redwood National Park, California.

Birch in the Northeast

The Northeast of the United States has its alders too, but here birches are more dominant and furnish similar landscapes that are just as magnificent. The two most common birches are the paper birch (*Betula papyrifera*) and the gray birch (*B. populifolia*). No tree is more graceful than these, and no tree offers a whiter bark. As with alders, these birches grow happily in clumps and dense groves.

In the grove pictured in Plate 68, from Maine's Acadia National Park, the trees show different levels of organization: individual trunks are gathered into clumps, and the clumps are arranged so as to indicate a path. As with alders, the effect is one of rustic grace, natural but refined—and very inviting.

In spite of high praise from horticulturists for being a relatively disease-free and bug-free birch, the gray birch is seldom available through the nursery trade. Although no birch is better suited for the kind of treatment shown in this example from Acadia, the paper birch (*Betula papyrifera*) and the European white birch (*B. pendula*), in a non-weeping variety, are close seconds. In places where the bronze birch borer is a problem, the Japanese birch (*B. platyphylla* var. *japonica*) in the cultivar 'Whitespire' may be even better, although it is a larger tree and lacks the gracefulness of the others. Whatever the choice, any reasonable approximation is likely to give a cherished landscape.

Unfortunately, none of these trees is particularly happy far inland, where the air is dry, the sun unrelenting most of the year, and winter sees wrenching fluctuations in temperatures. What can carry such designs into regions like the American Midwest? We can think of only one candidate: aspen. Before we see how well aspen can be used to create similar effects, we will visit one more example of birch, this grove staged against the perfect backdrop.

Plate 68. Birch grove in Acadia National Park, Maine.

White Birch, Black Cliffs

They are thought to be ancient sea cliffs, those black ramparts of rock traversed by the Gorham Mountain Trail in Maine's Acadia National Park, and ancient they appear. Their surfaces are well-eroded, with no sharp edges or signs of recent cleavage as is so apparent in much of the stone found elsewhere in the park. These cliffs are now far beyond the reach of the sea, and where soil has accumulated, trees and shrubs have taken root.

From the very start of the trail, the landscape is wondrous, but where the white trunks of gray birch (*Betula populifolia*) stand in front of the black cliffs, the landscape takes on an almost surreal aspect (Plate 69). The contrast is so stark and the patterns so well-defined that the effect is stunning. Only the green leaves lend color to the otherwise black-and-white theme. The scene has a timelessness about it—the ancient rock, the young birch—that makes it unforgettable.

We have hiked this trail only three times—not enough, not nearly enough. What pleasure it would bring to be able to see this landscape whenever we wanted to. Were it only a garden, a domesticated garden, our garden!

Unfortunately, few of us have an ancient sea cliff to incorporate in a landscape. Something of similar effect might be achieved by substituting some other backdrop for the cliff, something dark enough and featureless enough to set off the whiteness of the birch bark and the linear pattern of the trunks. Of course, a large stone wall would do, or a darkly painted building. A living wall could also serve the purpose, one of English or Baltic ivy (*Hedera helix*), dense and dark. Or the living wall could be a stand of evergreens, some smallish dark green cultivar of spruce (*Picea*), or hemlock (*Tsuga*), or best of all, yew (*Taxus*). Will any of these choices come close to the model? Not really, but they might honor the spirit of the original: a dark backdrop to display the elegant white tree trunks. In lieu of the real thing, it will have to do, and it will do quite nicely.

As for the birch, you could use the same gray birch or another white-barked one like the paper birch (*Betula papyrifera*), the European white birch (*B. pendula*), or whitespire Japanese birch (*B. platyphylla* var. *japonica* 'Whitespire'). Even aspen (*Populus tremuloides*) could be enlisted. In any case, the result, although only an approximation of the original, should be stunningly beautiful.

Plate 69. White birch and black cliffs along Gorham Mountain Trail, Acadia National Park, Maine.

Aspen in the Midwest

Over much of the Midwest, neither red alder nor the white-barked birches flourish. It's too dry, too windy, the snow cover is too unreliable, and usually the soil is insufferably alkaline. But there is an alternative: aspen (*Populus tremuloides*) succeeds where these others do not. In many respects, it's the design equivalent of the other two: slender boled, graceful, and happy growing in clumps and dense groves. The aspen's bark may not be as white as the birch's or as ornate as the alder's, but it is more than striking, and the golden fall color is upstaged by none. But again, we must remind the gardener that aspen, like birch and alder, is short-lived, susceptible to disease, and a magnet for insects. Fortunately, it grows like a weed and suckers with the slightest nick of the roots, so a grove is easily encouraged to rejuvenate itself. Young saplings growing vigorously beside their elders creates a delightful effect. This is common in the forest but not in the garden, where new volunteers are too often viewed as trespassers—too bad, since the young trees are even more graceful than the adults and fill the scene with a sense of vigor and renewal. This is how we like to see them, growing together in a variety of sizes and ages, and this is how we grow them in our own garden (see Plate 106).

With only a couple of examples it is impossible to even hint at the beauty and wide-ranging variety of effects to be seen in aspen forests. So we indulged our love for these forests by including several. Still, the selections in no way capture the wealth of design ideas to be found in visiting forests of aspen.

Gilding an Autumn Temple

Nowhere does the show of autumn gold surpass that staged in the Rocky Mountains. Nowhere in the Rockies is there a better place to view it than in Rocky Mountain National Park. And nowhere in the park is the display more spectacular than along Cub Lake Trail (Plate 70). Here you do not find the kaleidoscope of autumn color that is seen on the East Coast, or even elsewhere in the park, where autumn flares up in brilliant patches of oranges, reds, and purples conferred by sumac (*Rhus*), currant (*Ribes*), mountain ash (*Sorbus scopulina*), cliff jamesia (*Jamesia americana*), grouseberry (*Vaccinium scoparium*), and others. But along Cub Lake Trail, the golden leaves, white trunks, and gray rock set against a blue sky is striking enough, to be certain, and what might be lost in color variety is more than gained in coherence and harmony. At a spot within a half mile of the lake, the straight trunks of aspen are massed like the columns of a Greek temple, and in autumn, like a temple with a golden floor and a golden dome. Every September, hordes of the faithful make their pilgrimage to see the wonder. We photographed this stand at its finest hour, but a grove of aspen is an attraction throughout the year, in leaf or deciduated.

Although aspen is the only tree playing a major role in this example, there is nothing at all monotonous about it. More than enough interest is generated by the placement of the trees. Isolated specimens, pairs, clumps with several trunks—all seem to be arranged in a completely logical, yet unpredictable pattern. It is this elusive coherence that makes this landscape so fascinating. This

Plate 70. Golden temple of aspen, Cub Lake Trail, Rocky Mountain National Park, Colorado.

effect of planned randomness characterizes many of our favorite landscapes. How did the arrangement get to be as it is? How could it possibly have been different? It is a game of chance with a perfect outcome, and that is the wonder of it all.

A section of garden modeled after this spot along Cub Lake Trail would be easy to design. Aspen, both nursery-grown and collected, are readily available and inexpensive. The trees pictured here are full grown, but aspen reaches maturity very quickly, and even young trees have the greenish white bark and fall color of the adults. It is a good choice for zones 3 and 4 and mountain communities; warmer climates and lower altitudes do not suit it as well, and under these cushier conditions aspen is more prone to disease and insect attack, and the tree may not show the glorious fall color for which it is so renowned.

In sites that are lower and warmer, birch can be an alternative and will fare better. Birch has many of the same shortcomings as aspen, however, and a few additional ones as well. Nevertheless, where adapted, and where they can be given adequate care, these trees will contribute their unique grace, bark, and fall color to make a landscape of incomparable elegance and beauty.

Walk Through a Golden Curtain

Early October in Colorado's highcountry: Indian summer, brilliant blue skies, shirtsleeve temperatures—and aspen in full color. The glorious show is at its peak at an elevation of 10,000 ft (3,050 m), near Bear Lake in Rocky Mountain National Park. One of the trails there leads through a particularly fine stand, curtain after curtain of pure glittering gold (Plate 71). We make our pilgrimage here every year, but there aren't enough years in a lifetime to embrace the beauty of this place.

How long does the show last? It depends on the largess of the weather—it can last nearly a month in a good year—but the beauty extends beyond the main attraction. The prelude is itself a joy, as the dark green summer leaves turn to a more translucent lime-green, an effect that recalls the sparkle of spring's flush of new growth. The encore to the fall show is also a treat: bare of leaves, it's a study in line and rhythm, a spare and exquisite effect that carries interest through the winter.

What a joy it would be to have a landscape like this where you could see it whenever you wished, in every season of the year. Unfortunately, domesticating this scene presents some potential problems above and beyond those that beset aspen in particular. Of a more general nature is a problem that concerns any garden that consists primarily of trees (or other plants) of a single species. If the species is susceptible to attack by insects or disease, the infestation or infection of one tree can rapidly spread to the others. If the condition is lethal, the entire planting may be lost. Unfortunately, it is the homogeneity that gives this type of landscape its cohesion and accounts for much of its impact and appeal. Until we have stronger, more disease-resistant cultivars to choose from, we will have to suffer the shortcomings of these trees as best we can—their effect in the landscape is that singular, that spectacular.

Plate 71. Walk through a golden curtain, near Bear Lake in Rocky Mountain National Park, Colorado.

Mountainside Aspen

The Bierstadt Lake Trail in Colorado's Rocky Mountain National Park is pleasant enough with its views of Longs Peak, Hallett Peak, and Flattop Mountain. The lake at its terminus is also pleasant, although unremarkable by the high standards of the highcountry hereabouts. But a third of the way up the ascent, a hillside of aspen offers such singular beauty that it draws us to this trail again and again (Plate 72).

It's a young grove on meager and gravelly soil, but the trees twist and bend as though burdened by great age. They lean outward from the hill and then arch backward, reaching for light. Sunlight they have enough of, but perhaps not enough water or soil to give them the rapid straight growth we see in cushier situations. The conditions of the mountainside—the harsh sun, extreme wind, and short growing season—forces the trees into a tighter, slower, less succulent habit of growth, which may position them for greater longevity and greater resistance to pests and diseases. In years with uncommonly abundant rainfall, other stands of aspen will have their leaves change from green to brown, and then deciduate (a fungus is the cause). But this mountainside grove colors up faithfully and brilliantly, a reliable spectacle every autumn.

Perhaps the main point of this example is to show that there is an alternative to designing with trees that are canonically upright and straight, shaped in the lollipop mode for the convenience of the nursery trade. Growing them with a bit of tough love, with a bend and a twist, not only might make for a more interesting stand but may encourage longevity and discourage certain pests and diseases. Maybe this is heretical, but it has worked for bonsai growers over the centuries.

Plate 72. Mountainside aspen, Bierstadt Lake Trail, Rocky Mountain National Park, Colorado.

White on White: Aspen in Winter

After the golden leaves are shed, what interest does a grove of aspen offer? Come the first snow, the riot of color staged at the end of the growing season is repainted in shades of white alone, ever so subtle, ever so striking (Plate 73). Now the linear pattern of the trees against the snow is the main attraction. Depth of field is hard to discern in the flat lighting of an overcast day, and the forest takes on a two-dimensional aspect. Standing in front of the grove, the trees seem to form an almost solid screen, as effective a backdrop as any garden wall in Kyoto, be it of stone or bamboo. Yet the aspen are placed far enough apart from one another to allow the visitor to stroll between them and enjoy their company. In a large stand, the white trunks surrounding you on all sides, the effect is surreal, disorienting, with only your own tracks to lead you out. But you want to stay, to fully experience the profound solitude and beauty of this place. Gray skies and the cold light of winter emphasize the monochrome aspect and enhance the mood. Whatever the temperature, it's cold, it's silent, it's winter. We love it, these dormant trees, this forest carved out of ivory, this abstract piece of landscape art.

Months will pass before the creamy white trunks begin to show a tinge of gray-green, the first signs of life reawakening. And then it will take only a few warm nights and a few long days for the trees to cover themselves with a shiny new mantle of translucent leaves, shimmering in the sun as they flutter in the slightest breeze. Through spring the pale green leaves darken and their undersides turn blue-gray as they harden. By summer, the translucence is almost gone, and the bicoloration emphasizes the fluttering of the leaves—trembling aspen.

Again, we must say that we love this tree, this weedy, short-lived, disease- and insect-prone tree; and we love the forests it makes. No tree is more graceful or more elegant. Junk tree though it is, aspen is unbeatable for its four seasons of interest and for the dramatic new face it presents in celebration of each. What a pity that it's such a damn nuisance.

Plate 73. Winter aspen, Timber Lake Trail, Rocky Mountain National Park, Colorado.

MIXED HARDWOODS: A Symphony of Line, Form, and Color

For interest born of variety, nothing quite equals a forest of mixed hardwoods. Oak, birch, beech, elm, and maple intermingled above an understory of azalea, holly, mountain laurel, and viburnum creates a luxuriance of growth that seems almost tropical. Exuberance fits the picture—pure exuberance. No one walks through such a forest without tapping some of the excitement and energy.

A forest of mixed hardwoods is a joy in every season, and is dramatically different in every season. Different species leaf out at different times, so the bright green wake-up hues of spring span nearly two months, with new leaves of one tree unfurling against the linear pattern of still-dormant neighbors. Scarcely have all the leaves hardened to the heat of summer when the autumn show begins—a spectacle renowned the world over. The display lingers for weeks, slowly ripening to full brilliance. Then it begins to mellow to more subtle hues. Various species color up at different times, and they shed their leaves at different times, so at the end of the season, the forest opens somewhat to show its underlying linear structure, while the few remaining leaves add sparks of color to the scene.

Maples are prime candidates for a forest of mixed hardwoods. Snakebark maples, like David maple (*Acer davidii*) and moosewood (*A. pensylvanicum*), have dark trunks lined in white that make a striking display against the snow. The fall color of these is muted, at least by the standards set by other maples. The moosewood has coarse or bold leaves, depending on how you see it; the leaves of the others are rather unremarkable in shape and in size. There is nothing coarse about the Japanese maple (*A. palmatum*), and its fall color is anything but muted. Cultivars are available that will end the season with a splash of gold, others with red. Some carry these colors into winter on their bark. Add to these options a variety of sizes and graceful silhouettes, fair shade tolerance, and a willingness to grow in dense stands, and you have in this one species a diversity of forms of unlimited applicability. Several varieties of the fullmoon maple (*A. japonicum*), the Oregon vine maple (*A. circinatum*), and the red maple (*A. rubrum*) are also excellent choices. The red maple is a larger tree that is often grown as an isolated specimen, but it is quite happy growing in a grove, where its height is more restricted. Hedge maple (*A. campestre*) with yellow fall color, Shantung maple (*A. truncatum*) with purple fall color, and bigtooth maple (*A. grandidentatum*) with colors from pale yellow to rich orange are others to consider in zones 4 to 7; the big-tooth is a particular favorite of ours. Where the planting has to contend with the conditions of zone 3 or 4, the Siberian maple (*A. ginnala*) is the one to use. This tree has far fewer cultivars than the Japanese maple, but the fall color of the species is magnificent, ultimately turning a deep red.

Of course, maples alone will not give the effect of the mixed hardwood forest. Add some white-barked birch to the maples and imagine the contrast and complement of forms, bark, and fall color. Or consider clumps of birch interplanted with sourwood (*Oxydendrum arboreum*), dogwood (*Cornus*), *Franklinia*, *Stewar-*

tia, redbud (*Cercis*), or witchhazel (*Hamamelis*). All these trees are of modest size. The last two turn yellow in the fall; the others will give you that autumn kick of scarlet that is so helpful in keeping the spirit alive through winter. And all have flowers of extraordinary beauty.

Other trees have splendid fall color with a more or less restrained curtain opener of translucent lime-green. Aspen (*Populus tremuloides*), for zones 2 to 6, must be mentioned, but with the usual caveats. Sweet gum (*Liquidambar styraciflua*), for zones 5 to 9, is another candidate, but the heavier leaves show less translucence. *Sassafras albidum* is a more unusual choice in zones 4 to 9, but it may be too brittle for regions of high wind and heavy snow.

For the understory of a private forest, one can choose from among azalea (*Rhododendron*), mountain laurel (*Kalmia*), Japanese andromeda (*Pieris japonica*), and *Enkianthus*; flowering currant (*Ribes sanguineum*) or clove currant (*R. odoratum*); *Fothergilla*, various viburnums, and many others that provide both spring flowers and fall color. Or maybe use some of these as highlights to punctuate an evergreen groundcover like a spreading juniper (*Juniperus*) or creeping grapeholly (*Mahonia repens*). For a tall groundcover or a spot planting in a woodland setting, there is no better choice than ferns, although umbrella plant (*Peltiphyllum peltatum*), *Hosta*, *Epimedium*, and wild ginger (*Asarum*), among others, can also be used effectively.

With such a tempting selection of plants, some care and restraint has to be exercised to avoid a hodgepodge, a structureless mixture of trees and shrubs that pushes naturalness to the un-kempt, and the untamed to the disheveled. Here lies the challenge: mix the species, but create form and maintain structure within the variety. Not an easy assignment in a small space, but when it works, how rewarding it is. And remember that the mixed forest offers horticultural advantages. Many insect pests and diseases are host specific, and their spread is facilitated in sites where a single species is dominant. So mix and match—variety distinguishes these landscapes, and variety makes them perennially exciting.

A few maples (*Acer*) in a small bit of forest in New Hampshire.

Autumn Prelude

It takes nature time to paint an autumn canvas with the rich palette of saturated color that we see in Plates 76 and 77. Shorter days and cooler temperatures start the magical transformation. The full fiery display builds slowly through modulations of softer hues, the translucent pale yellows and lime-greens, hues that look back to spring rather than to the color festival ahead. It's an interlude that lasts only a couple of weeks, an interlude that is serene, yet filled with anticipation. The effect is widespread in the temperate zone, but nowhere is it more reliable or more splendid than in the forests of New Hampshire's White Mountains (Plate 74).

Perhaps the display is too short-lived to be a major concern, but it is such a singular event that it is worth marking the calendar to make certain it is not missed. But be careful! You might be so taken with it that you decide to spare no effort or expense to re-create the effect in your garden. Happily, bringing it into your garden does not involve major expenditures of any kind, provided you live in a zone between 3 and 7. In climates where trees do not deciduate, it may be best to contact a travel agent before September.

Where the effect can be achieved, a broad selection of superb trees will serve it up, trees that not only will supply the lime-green translucence of our example, but will offer a full four seasons of landscape interest. Maples have to be ranked at the top of the list, but there are many others, and many shrubs to accompany the trees (as discussed in the previous section). With a careful choice of plant material, the effect illustrated from the White Mountains can be attained in a modest amount of space and in a modest amount of time. True, it's a fleeting effect—two weeks or maybe three and it's gone—but this only adds to its appeal and guarantees that we will never see enough of it, even if it is part of our garden.

Plate 74. Autumn prelude in New Hampshire's White Mountains.

A Gentle Harmony of Autumn Color

Autumn comes gently to Falling Waters Trail in Franconia Notch State Park, in New Hampshire's White Mountains. Shorter days and a gradual chill rework the color scheme, changing green to a subtle mix of golden hues, from soft yellow to tawny brown. Occasionally, a shout of orange or even scarlet comes through, but nothing loud enough to break the gentle harmony of browns and golds. When other forests in New England are blaring a color blast to close the season, this forest brings the curtain down with quiet dignity (Plate 75). Perhaps not as exciting as some other autumn displays, this one may be more deeply satisfying.

Achieving such a quiet harmony of fall color requires some planning, since so many cultivars of trees and shrubs that have been selected for their autumn display have been chosen to give the brightest, brashest, brassiest color possible. And, of course, we do not want the garden to embarrass us during the other seasons. Even with these restrictions, however, we have many choices for plants that will give subtle autumn hues, complement each other, and be an asset to the garden all year long.

Of the woody plants to be seen along Falling Waters Trail, many are well-suited for a garden rendition of this example, though others are too rank and weedy when taken under cultivation. Some trees to consider include moosewood (*Acer pensylvanicum*), yellow birch (*Betula alleghaniensis*), sweet birch (*B. lenta*), eastern redbud (*Cercis canadensis*), American beech (*Fagus grandifolia*), green ash (*Fraxinus pennsylvanica*), and basswood linden (*Tilia americana*).

Among the shrub candidates are summersweet (*Clethra alnifolia*), witchhazel (*Hamamelis virginiana*), and several of the deciduous azaleas or rhododendrons (*Rhododendron*). In a dense planting, where shade tolerance of the shorter trees and shrubs is a must, any of these shrubs make excellent choices. Redbud grows to a lean and lanky 30 ft (9 m) in the midst of other trees, colors a soft yellow in autumn, and offers a knockout display of fuchsia blossoms in the spring; cultivars also come with pink and white blossoms, for those with sensitive retinas. Witchhazel will give a spring preview of yellow, orange, or red spidery blossoms in the middle of winter, as well as soft yellow fall foliage (although some cultivars turn more red or orange than yellow). Redbud and witchhazel both have bold foliage, the leaves big enough to be considered coarse by some. Summersweet, true to its name, offers deliciously sweet-scented panicles of white or pink blossoms in early summer. The azaleas flower in spring, and several also boast highly fragrant blooms.

Of course, where these plants are unavailable or are unsuited to the climate, one can choose from many non-native alternatives. For example, lacebark elm (*Ulmus parvifolia*) is an ideal candidate, a rather small and slender elm to 50 ft (15 m), with a most interesting bark pattern and muted yellow to purple fall color. Some of the maples, such as hedge maple (*Acer campestre*), might be of use, but many of the others are just too flamboyant for the application at hand. The Japanese rose (*Kerria japonica*) belongs to the rose family, but it is not a rose; it has single or double, yellow or white

Plate 75. A gentle harmony of autumn colors along Falling Waters Trail in Franconia Notch State Park, New Hampshire.

flowers in mid-spring, soft yellow fall color, and bright green branches right through winter. Any of these choices can be grown in zones 4 through 7. In warmer climates, fall color of the kind we see here is not expected. But if a true winter is the price you have to pay for a true fall, it's not a bad deal.

A Hint of Forest

As colorful as autumn is in the notches of New Hampshire, it is still a treat to see a splash of clear, singing red. As effective as a stoplight, a splash of red will cause drivers to slam on the brakes, swerve onto the shoulder, abandon their car, and bolt for a snapshot of the spectacle. Fortunately, these forest paparazzi never stay long, and within a few minutes are back in their car, tooling along the road in search of another patch of red, or a deer, or a squirrel, or an outhouse.

We were in Crawford Notch among our fellow paparazzi in just such pursuits when we spotted a bit of red forest. But this bit of red was neither large enough nor blaring enough to cause a traffic jam, and we were the only ones abandoning a car to capture the effect. What we found was much more than just a chromatic kick. Here, nature had composed a fragment of forest into a scene fit for the finest garden.

Within 20 ft (6 m) of the road, backed by a stream, was a narrow strip of forest, mostly red maples (*Acer rubrum*) in glorious fall color (Plate 76). The sun shone through the leaves and set them aglow. The trunks of these young trees appeared black in the light.

An occasional gray birch (*Betula populifolia*) displayed its white trunk in contrast to the red and black. The grove was thin, only a few trees deep, and the branching pattern of the maples was also thin, so the water could be seen through the stand. The delicate tracery of color and line gave the scene a distinctly oriental aspect—beauty compressed onto a single plane, like a Japanese screen painting.

How large does a stand of trees have to be in order to suggest a forest? How wide, how deep, how many species need it contain to be convincing? The Crawford Notch example shows that little space is needed in order to represent a forest in a manner that is completely enthralling. Here, only a few trees of only two species, thinly spaced and thinly branched, carry the design with extraordinary grace and effectiveness. It's the spare use of materials and space that recommends this nature scene as part of a garden design. It is small enough to be set against a wall or fence. On the other hand, there is enough integrity in the design to allow an expanded version to be used as a backdrop to a garden. In either application, it is likely to be one of the favorite parts of the garden; and during a month or so in the fall, it is likely to outshine everything else.

If using young trees, such a feature is easy to set in place. Nursery-grown maples and birches are readily available. Although red maple will eventually be too large and massive for most sites, there are many cultivars of Japanese maple (*Acer palmatum*) and full-moon maple (*A. japonicum*) that could be used instead. Hardy in zones 5 through 8, these are even more elegant in form, more amenable to pruning, and more spectacular in fall color than red maple. In regions as cold as zone 3, the Siberian maple (*A. ginnala*)

Plate 76. Hint of forest in Crawford Notch State Park, New Hampshire.

could be used. But a word of caution about this often-recommen-ded tree: it is relatively brittle and is highly susceptible to breakup under a heavy snow load.

Paper birch (*Betula papyrifera*) or European white birch (*B. pendula*) are two of several birches that could be used as well as gray birch. Here we have a range of hardiness from zone 3 through zone 7, but we must remember that most birches have more than their share of bugs and diseases. This is also true of aspen (*Populus tremuloides*), although it might be an acceptable substitute for birch in certain climates. Our first choice is the one nature used in the example: birch and maple.

A Private Forest in Autumn

Can a private garden really contain a bit of forest? Absolutely, as our example from Amherst, Massachusetts, shows (Plate 77). The forest serves as a background to the garden and as a screen from the road behind it. The foreground of this landscape is nothing more than an expanse of lawn on a gently sloping hillside. But when autumn comes to New England, this little forest of mostly maple trees erupts into a carnival of color: scarlet, orange, yellow, and remnants of green. It's a display that lasts the better part of a month, vibrant and vivid as any seen in nature. At this time of the year, the grass is completely hidden under a carpet of golden leaves. The color of the background is so intense and so varied that nothing else is needed to complete the composition; indeed, nothing could

be added to the design that could hold its own against the flamboyant display of the trees.

During other seasons so much lawn might be just so much lawn—a nuisance to maintain and a bore to look at. For spring and summer interest, more might be wanted. It is easy to imagine this stretch of foreground as a meadow awash with flowers: from late February into May, a sea of naturalized bulbs, snowdrops (*Galanthus*), hyacinths (*Hyacinthus*), and many daffodils (*Narcissus*); and from May to September, lupines (*Lupinus*), flax (*Linum*), California poppy (*Eschscholzia*), dame's rocket (*Hesperis matronalis*), yarrow (*Achillea*), Jupiter's beard (*Centranthus ruber*), *Veronica*, *Salvia*, and all sorts of plants from the daisy family, including *Aster*, *Echinacea*, *Helianthus*, and *Rudbeckia*. For the autumn meadow, *Anemone*, *Aster*, or *Chrysanthemum*, choosing cultivars that retain some of the unassuming grace of their species forebears, might contribute additional interest. But again, the autumn display could well be left to the trees.

At the edge of the forest, we might place some spring-flowering trees and shrubs: azaleas and rhododendrons (*Rhododendron*), *Fothergilla*, *Enkianthus*, mountain laurel (*Kalmia*), Japanese andromeda (*Pieris japonica*), *Viburnum*, dogwoods (*Cornus*), flowering apricots, cherries, and plums (*Prunus*), crabapples (*Malus*), and hawthorns (*Crataegus*) are just a few of the candidates. Many of these will also be players in the fall festival, contributing their share of brilliant foliage color. The trees can be chosen to give us as outrageously flamboyant an autumn display as possible. Maple (*Acer*)

Plate 77. Private forest, Amherst, Massachusetts.

comes to mind first as a key player, offering many varieties, shapes, and colors. *Sassafras*, sweet gum (*Liquidambar*), mountain ash (*Sorbus*), witchhazel (*Hamamelis*), and serviceberry (*Amelanchier*) are among the many other candidates. Maybe the more subtle hues of birch (*Betula*), ash (*Fraxinus*), or elm (*Ulmus*) would serve to moderate the display while setting off the more brazen players. But an autumn extravaganza is the point of this example, and any talk of moderation will come only from those too timid or conservative to entertain such a bold blast of color.

Most of the plants suggested are hardy from zone 4 to zone 7 and above, although in the warmer zones such extravagant fall color is much less likely. However, some of the Japanese maples (*Acer palmatum*), fullmoon maples (*A. japonicum*), sweetgum, eastern flowering dogwood (*Cornus florida*), and others are fairly dependable even in zones 7 and 8.

Crystal Palace

Winter does not drive the beauty from a hardwood forest, but it does alter its expression dramatically. Where only weeks before the first snow the scene was painted in bold, contrasting swatches of high-key hues, the emphasis now turns to linear patterns in close color harmonies. Black trees against white snow, branches and twigs highlighted in silver frost—it's a quieter, more subtle, and maybe more moving scene that does not hide the chill of winter or even soften it. Instead, it highlights the exquisite beauty of the season. On a gray day in the middle of January, traveling on cross-country skis in Northfield, Massachusetts, we found ourselves in just such a crystal palace (Plate 78). It was all texture and reflection and refraction; and the magic of it made us forget the temperature.

To design such a landscape, or to put it more modestly, to design a landscape through which nature can present such an effect, does not require a great amount of space or a great amount of patience. The choice of trees is important, however. They have to be somewhat shade tolerant and able to grow in dense groves. They should branch well, retain a slender habit, and have a straight trunk. With other seasons in mind, you might also ask for a variety of interesting leaf patterns, quiet or raucous fall color, or even a display of flowers during some season. Candidates for such a winter display with amenities throughout the year include various maples, such as red maple (*Acer rubrum*), sugar maple (*A. saccharum*), and Shantung maple (*A. truncatum*), among others. The Shantung maple is a particular favorite of ours, considerably smaller at 25 ft (7.5 m), with the expected maple-shaped leaves. A small elm, such as the lacebark elm (*Ulmus parvifolia*), would be a nice addition. The flowering component might be the plum *Prunus nigra* 'Princess Kay' or a flowering cherry, such as Sargent's cherry (*P. sargentii*). *Prunus sargentii* is hardy into zone 4 and has superb bark, superb pink blossoms, and superb fall color. It is somewhat shade tolerant and can be had in a fastigiate cultivar. We can think of no better flowering tree for this application.

An understory of shrubs might be added, and there are many from which to choose. Azalea (*Rhododendron*), andromeda (*Pieris*),

Plate 78. Crystal palace in Northfield, Massachusetts.

holly (*Ilex*), grapeholly (*Mahonia*), mountain laurel (*Kalmia*), and viburnum (*Viburnum*) are all shade tolerant, attractive all year long, and superb in at least one season. If a winter effect similar to that shown in Plate 78 is the top priority, however, then it may be best to do without shrubs altogether. In that way, the strong, uncluttered, linear element of the design will be emphasized, and it is the line and its stark contrast against the snow that gives this landscape its character.

EVERGREEN FORESTS

Evergreen conifers maintain a complete presence in the landscape whatever the season—an important consideration in climates where winter keeps other trees stripped to their bare bones for nearly half a year. Yet, some people identify evergreen with ever-the-same. They think of the effect as monotonous, and maybe too heavy in its unrelenting persistence. But this is largely a misperception, as evergreens, particularly in the temperate regions, interact with the seasons to create an extraordinary range of extraordinary effects. Come spring, pines, firs, and spruces candle out in the brightest and lightest hues of yellow, blue, or green, the new growth perfectly set off by the dark foliage of past years. The attitude and color of these candles is the very embodiment of the latent energy of the season. By summer, the candles have hardened, and the branches assume a more relaxed position. Fall brings modest changes, as the overall color modulates to quieter tones. During winter, the trees don't change much at all, but the snow works its magic, transforming them into free-form sculptures, while hoarfrost flecks the trees with platinum. It's almost enough to make you wish that spring would be delayed for another month or so.

Nevertheless, even with these seasonal changes, a homogeneous stand of evergreens can be monotonous—too much of not enough. With some, like the standard-size cultivars of spruce, fir, and hemlock, the form is so upright and proper, so canonically conical, that they show little variation, except for size and sometimes color. This homogeneity is fine for stands that serve as windbreaks and barriers, but dull and boring as a landscape. But place groups of evergreens in an irregular pattern, wind a walk among the groups, intersperse some shrubs and perennials that tolerate shade and acidic soil (for acidic it will become) and you create a private haven of all-season interest. Even the distinctive pungent fragrance of this kind of forest is something to covet.

Garden Version of an Evergreen Forest

A gentle stream meandering through a stand of blue spruce—it's a common but always welcome scene in the montane region of the Rockies. Most blue spruces in the wild are green, but occasionally one finds a small grove of "shiners," silvery blue-gray specimens on which the shiny needles give the trees an ethereal glow even in dim light. In a small evergreen stand, like the one pictured here in Plate 79, the effect is anything but heavy or somber. The color and texture of the foliage, the jaunty attitude of the young trees, and the sparkling stream will brighten any mood.

Plate 79. Garden version of an evergreen forest in Aurora, Colorado.

But this scene is not one surrounded by mountains. Instead, it's surrounded by apartment buildings in Aurora, Colorado, part of a small park built for the residents (also see Plate 65). And it must be greatly appreciated, for in spite of the hundreds of people that have access to it, it shows no signs of misuse or neglect.

The very limitations of the site, the small size of the plot and the need to have a composition that could be viewed and enjoyed from many different angles, encouraged a design that was somewhat open and uses few trees. The heaviness and homogeneity that so often comes with an extensive use of evergreens were completely avoided.

Blue spruce (*Picea pungens*) is one of the most popular of all landscape trees and is widely available in nurseries from zone 3 to zone 7. Some say that it is too popular, too common, and ultimately too large growing for most gardens; they point out the tree's habit of growing old gracelessly; and they rightfully criticize the well-worn visual cliché of planting a single blue spruce in the middle of the front lawn and allowing it to grow to monstrous size. In this example, however, the trees are planted in a grove, and although only a few trees are used, obvious symmetries have been avoided, creating a composition that is unlikely to bore you no matter how many times you see it.

For a small site, you can choose dwarf cultivars of spruce. Several are available that will slowly grow to a mature height of less than 24 ft (7.2 m), while retaining their shapeliness for a long, long time. Of course, most of these cultivars are blue—about as striking a blue as a blue spruce can be, and that's blue. On the other hand, these are slow-growing enough to make you aware of the finiteness of your life and your bank account.

Only two other trees come close to the color and stateliness of blue spruce: white fir (*Abies concolor*) and atlas cedar (*Cedrus atlantica*). Dwarf blue cultivars of these are more difficult to obtain, and the cedar has a more rangy open shape that is perhaps better suited for specimen display. However, both have their advantages in climates where blue spruce is unhappy, climates that are too warm, too dry, or too muggy.

As common as blue spruce is, we see this landscape as uncommonly appealing: small enough for even a modest plot, beautiful in every season. It is a landscape that requires little upkeep and makes little demand of resources. In fact, it would rebel if you fussed over it too much. Spruce, fir, and cedar do not take kindly to the hedge clippers; heavy-handed pruning alters their shape and texture to a Chia Pet configuration. They are best left alone to grow as they please. Leave the clippers in the garage and pack a pocketful of peanuts to this garden—the squirrels and bluejays will thank you for the free lunch. And you get the equivalent of a gardener's free lunch: all the pleasure of a beautiful naturalistic landscape without the need of extensive maintenance.

Moss Forest

The high-seas highwaymen that plied their nefarious trade off Maine's coast took safe harbor in Somes Sound. There, within easy walking distance of the shore, they found a source of fresh water to fill their casks; and that is how Pirate's Spring got its name. Now the spring is the destination of landlubbers hiking along the sound in Acadia National Park. It's an extraordinarily varied and scenic trail even by the park's high standards, and it meanders from the water's edge into the forest and back again.

A most memorable section of the trail leads through a small opening in the forest along a poorly defined path of cobbles and flagstones through a deep carpet of brilliant green moss. In our photograph (Plate 80), a large gray boulder (the dot of red paint marks the trail) and the twin trunks of an old fir (*Abies*) centers the composition. It's a scene of idyllic beauty, one that speaks of repose and tranquility. The lushness of growth and the brilliant foliage color testify to the abundant moisture in the air as well as the soil. The arrangement of the elements in the overall scheme seems to suggest the intelligence and sensitivity of some master of landscape design, rather than nature's play of chance.

You move slowly through such a forest. You don't want to injure the moss, and the footing over moist rocks is none too secure. Most of all, you move slowly because the beauty of the place is overwhelming, and you want to take in as much of it as you can.

In spite of its unique beauty, this is not an exotic landscape. There are no strident colors and no unfamiliar forms. There are no unusual land formations, no strange trees, no bizarre flowers. In fact, all the plants we see here—the fir, the moss, and the ferns—are rather common, or at least have common look-alikes. Nor is the arrangement of the elements in any way singular. It is just that the organization of this landscape strikes the eye as being perfect—in perfect balance and in perfect harmony. It could not be more invit-

Plate 80. Moss forest along Pirate's Spring Trail, Acadia National Park, Maine.

179

ing or more soothing, and the lucky visitor takes part in the harmony.

The very lack of unusual features, plants, or landforms makes this an apt model for a cultivated garden. The boulders, essential as they are to the composition, are in no way unusual, and even cast stone can be used instead. Cultivars of various fir trees are widely available in a wide assortment of heights, but spruce (*Picea*), hemlock (*Tsuga*), or cedar (*Cedrus*) might also be used. The compositional effect of the double trunk of the tree in the center of the photo is an important design component, and since nursery-grown stock is usually grown to only one trunk and making multiple trunks takes time, it may be best to plant two trees for the purpose and plant them as close together as possible.

The only feature that inland gardeners will have to give some thought to replacing is the moss. After all, this landscape is bathed in moisture-laden air off the Atlantic Ocean, and inland gardens that seldom experience mists and have little rain will have to find a moss look-alike for a groundcover. But this is not a problem, for one can choose from among thyme (*Thymus*), *Sedum*, or creeping veronica (*Veronica repens*). Rupturewort (*Herniaria glabra*) is also a good choice, if you can tolerate the name. Corsican mint (*Mentha requienii*) is another candidate. The green Irish moss (*Sagina subulata* 'Verna') and the green-gold Scotch moss (*Sagina subulata* 'Aurea') are convincing moss look-alikes. All these succeed in zone 4, but the last two require a bit more water. In warmer zones, baby tears (*Soleirolia soleirolii*) will create a delightful mossy carpet, and it too is available in a green form and a yellow form. Even juniper is a candidate; some cultivars of *Juniperus horizontalis* barely reach a height of 2 in (5 cm) and have a distinctly mossy appearance.

All these alternatives have but one fault: none tolerates heavy foot-traffic. If heavy foot-traffic is what must be tolerated, bluegrass will have to do. At best, it's second best, but it will capture some of the spirit. And even the nuisance of a lawn would be worth the privilege of having a landscape like this one at your doorstep.

Moss Forest: A More Rugged View

Famed for its grand scenery on a monumental scale—its mountains, glaciers, and surging rivers—Canada's Jasper National Park also offers more gentle scenery of more modest dimensions. On the hills overlooking Johnston Canyon, we found another example of a forest on mossy ground (Plate 81), an example far different in spirit than the one just visited in Acadia National Park.

Here, black rock forms the substratum, and a very shallow topdressing of soil supports the forest. Yet, there is enough moisture for moss to grow, a moss of a harsher texture and not as verdant as that seen in the previous example. The dark, checkered bark of the trees, fir (*Abies*) or spruce (*Picea*), continues the theme, giving this moss forest a finely chiseled look.

The exposed black boulders certainly add strength to the composition, but they are by no means essential to the effect. And the trees are small; except for the rough bark, they appear to be youngsters, although this may be an illusion—the harsh climate, short growing season, and scarcity of soil conspiring to dwarf what

Plate 81. Rugged moss forest, Johnston Canyon, Jasper National Park, Canada.

would be a much larger tree if grown elsewhere. These aspects of the landscape—its simplicity, its lack of large trees, its independence of large boulders—make it a workable garden model, especially for a hillside sloping up from the main viewpoints. The model even suggests a path leading from the center foreground back between the trees, although true moss and even the moss substitutes suggested in the previous section will not tolerate much foot traffic. In zone 6 or warmer climates, *Zoysia* could provide the harsher texture and duller color of the true moss; zoysias require very little maintenance and can be walked on.

No doubt, this landscape is not to everyone's taste. It has a rugged, almost scruffy individuality that may strike some as the antithesis of a moss garden. But for the designer who wants something bold and different, something handsome rather than pretty, this might be just the model.

BROADLEAF AGAINST CONIFER: The Ultimate in Contrast

Contrast is the key to landscapes of drama and excitement, and contrast is what you see when nature juxtaposes broadleaf deciduous trees against evergreen conifers—contrast in form, color, and texture. Is there a more effective foil for the blossoms of dogwood, cherry, or crabapple than a near-black backdrop of conifers? Can fall color be displayed more vividly than against evergreens? Even summer leaves stand out effectively against the much darker needles. In winter, the conifers seem darker still as the white-bark boles of aspen, birch, and alder positively gleam against them. Deciduous against evergreen: it's a design strategy that guarantees spectacular effects throughout the year.

In planning a high-contrast garden with deciduous and evergreen trees, the special requirements of the two groups have to be considered. Most evergreen conifers grow much more slowly than deciduous trees. This presents a problem if the conifers are to be used as a background, and it requires care in the selection and pruning of the deciduous trees. Even if the intended effect is not obtained immediately, however, the intermediate stages of growth will also give a great deal of pleasure.

Spruce (*Picea*), fir (*Abies*), hemlock (*Tsuga*), and pine (*Pinus*) are primary candidates for the evergreen components of the design, and often they are mentioned together as being visually equivalent; but there are essential differences in their landscape effect. Spruce, fir, and hemlock are usually seen as cone-shaped trees growing with a single leader. Limiting their height or imposing on them a different shape through pruning is not easy and often results in a contrivance that is as ungainly as it is unnatural. Spruce and fir tend to take on a disheveled appearance as they age, more frumpy than picturesque, with lower branches limp and nearly bare. On the other hand, if a garden is planned for only a single lifetime of beauty, spruce and fir will do quite nicely, and these trees offer several advantages. When young and furnished with branches from the ground up, the lower branches serve as a groundcover. This removes the necessity (as well as the opportunity and pleasure) of planting beneath them.

By contrast, pines assume a variety of shapes as they mature. Such variety gives the trees their individuality and makes it easy to control their height while enhancing their character by pruning. Many species of pines are soon tall enough that one can prune away their lower branches, which provides sheltered microclimates under the trees in which many shrubs, ferns, and other groundcovers thrive.

There are other differences to consider. The cone-shaped fir, spruce, and hemlock allow more light to penetrate the upper reaches of the planting, an important advantage for the deciduous trees that are planted among them. As a group, they also are more tolerant of shade than most pines (one usually finds pines on south-facing slopes, and spruce and fir on north-facing slopes). These are attributes worth considering, especially if an evergreen stand is wanted as a background, one that is dense enough to serve as a visual screen or a sound barrier. But even when spruce, fir, or hemlock are used, it is important to ensure that the deciduous elements get their share of sunlight. This means either allowing more space between the deciduous trees and the evergreens, or planting the deciduous trees to the south or southwest of the evergreens. We have not mentioned certain other choices for the evergreen component of the design, either because of a limited range (true cedars [*Cedrus*]), or exceedingly slow growth (yew [*Taxus*]), or a habit that is too wide-spreading (true cedars again), or because they seem less suitable in shape (monkey puzzle tree [*Araucaria araucana*] and other *Araucaria*).

Even with these restrictions, high-contrast landscapes like those pictured here can be realized in zones 2 through 8, and there are enough suitable species to allow for all sorts of customization and personalization in the design. A high-contrast backyard forest? Why not?

Aspen and Pine: Two Views

Some of the most striking examples of high-contrast landscapes featuring evergreen and deciduous trees involve aspen or birch set against pine, spruce, fir, or hemlock. Even in the cold light of an overcast winter day, the contrast is stunning, with the conifers forming a near-black backdrop against which the white trunks of the deciduous trees are staged for maximum effect. The most striking display of all comes in autumn, when golden leaves dance against the dark blue-greens. It may not be enough to forestall the onslaught of winter, but its memory will keep the spirit warm for several months.

To see the play of aspen against evergreen conifers at its dramatic best, one has to visit Rocky Mountain National Park during the latter half of October. The park draws visitors by the millions, and they come in every season, but no season leaves them more ecstatic than autumn. Every year, the first frosts of fall start another gold rush, and the mobs descend on the park to witness the spectacle. As the color show makes its way down the mountains and into the valleys, its progress is chronicled by the press day-by-day. It's front-page news and boosts tourism nearly as much as the ski-slopes do.

Our first example is found a mere mile along the Finch Lake Trail in Rocky Mountain National Park—too bad, finding such beauty should be the reward of much more effort. The trail leads through a stand of aspen (*Populus tremuloides*) and ponderosa pine (*Pinus ponderosa*). The stand is fairly open, and the hiker can stroll between the trees and under the pines. Superb in all seasons, the grove reaches its full glory in autumn when golden leaves are set against the dark green conifers and the unbeatable blue of a Colorado sky (Plate 82). Even the forest floor turns golden under a carpet of fallen leaves. The show can go on for nearly a month, until the gold gives way to the linear pattern of white trunks against the nearly black color of the conifers. Then the snow comes and the scene is repainted to white on white, a study in elegant simplicity.

Plate 82. Aspen and pine off Finch Lake Trail in Rocky Mountain National Park, Colorado.

Another example, again from Rocky Mountain National Park, requires no walking at all. It is found along the side of the road that leads to Endovalley (Plate 83). A river runs parallel to the road and behind the stand. From river to road measures about 30 ft (9 m)—a distance that can be accommodated in a yard of modest size. Here is a wonderful example of what can be done in a narrow background. Notice the striking black ovals that decorate the lower 5 ft (1.5 m) of the trunks of the aspens: deer, porcupines, rabbits, and other wildlife forage on aspen bark during winter, and the wounds blacken as they heal. We find these bold patterns both interesting and beautiful, but they serve to remind us that aspen, birch, alder, and other trees with delicate ornamental bark are easily and permanently scarred, not only by beasts of the forest but by human vandals of the Jack-the-ripper mindset. Elsewhere in the park are stands of equally fine trees that have paid for their beauty with their hides, hideously scarred forever from ground level to as high as one can reach with a penknife. Why would someone come all the way here to do this? However, in spite of widespread depredation, many stands as fine as the one pictured here still remain—serene and stately, and as yet spared from the knife.

To translate this landscape to a cultivated garden requires only two species of trees: aspen and pine. As mentioned before, however, aspen does not perform well in many parts of the country. In places where aspen is too prone to insect attack, or disease, or does not show the fall color for which it is famous, birch (*Betula*) or alder (*Alnus*) may be a better choice. In the authors' garden in Boulder, Colorado, we have used aspen and pine extensively. Although ponderosa pine (*Pinus ponderosa*) is native to the nearby foothills and mountains, we chose Austrian pine (*Pinus nigra*) instead. Visually, the two are quite similar, though the needles of the ponderosa have a slightly yellowish cast, and the bark of mature trees is patterned like an alligator's hide, with auburn plates outlined in black. We choose the Austrian pine because of its resistance to the pine beetle and the devastating fungus that the beetle carries. As is sometimes the case, an exotic species may be the better choice in a certain site than a similar local one, either because of availability or resistance to diseases and insects of the region. This may seem heretical in these times when the "grow native" philosophy is being championed by so many horticulturists, but with a world of plants to choose from, the best choice may come from afar.

Plate 83. Aspen and pine, Endovalley, Rocky Mountain National Park, Colorado.

A study in platinum and black: a meadow of grasses in Cottonwood Park, Boulder, Colorado.

Chapter 7

DETAILS AND PRIVATE CORNERS

H<small>AIKU</small> is that pithy form of poetry perfected by the Japanese, a mere seventeen syllables in length, but rich in allusion and imagery. Sometimes a fragment of a landscape can be seen as visual haiku by evoking a mood or suggesting a larger theme. Even paths that lead to nature's grandest designs—paths along a coast, across a mountain ridge, or through a forest—are likely to offer all sorts of small details for which interest and beauty far exceed their size. Sometimes the effect is temporary, and sometimes it is a permanent part of the scene. The intimate scale of these details is emphasized by the bolder elements of the landscape, which in turn seem even grander by comparison. But often the details are as memorable as anything else seen along the trail.

A garden can also offer such features: vignettes of special interest, engaging small treasures to view up close and to linger over. In order to deliver their full effect, however, such features have to be properly staged and carefully integrated into the garden, where they will not only provide a focal point, but complement the overall design.

Not only do details add the finishing touches to a garden, but they also provide an opportunity to personalize the design and entertain interests and hobbies. Iris lovers can accent a path with some of their favorites; a shady corner can host a collection of primulas, or hostas; and those with a rock-strewn hillside can turn a curse into a blessing by creating a rockery.

One must remember, however, that no amount of detail will mask a poor garden design. At best, the detail can momentarily distract attention from the shortcomings of the overall scheme. But how tempting it is to attend to the details first and then worry about the larger structure of the garden. After all, it is easier to conceptualize the small-scale elements of a design; the cost is usually a fraction of that needed to realize the overall structure; it's physically easier to install a small-scale plan; and the desired effect can be obtained in a relatively short time. All of this encourages the common mistake of installing the details first, and then working around them to install the larger and more important design elements, a procedure that usually ends up costing more, taking more time and effort, and satisfying less. Nevertheless, details can add so much interest to a design that few gardens benefit by omitting them.

Nature provides us with so many examples of small-scale motifs that can be interpreted in a garden setting that it is impossible to even hint at the scope. At best, we can only point to a few that have enthralled us and that we would love to have in our own backyard. In fact, some of the examples we offer do come from our own backyard.

Bunchberry in Acadia National Park

In a secluded enclave within a hundred yards of the ocean in Maine's Acadia National Park, we found a superb stand of bunchberry dogwood (*Cornus canadensis*) (Plate 84). This diminutive relative of the eastern flowering dogwood (*Cornus florida*) stands at a height of only 8 in (20 cm), but its relation to the tree is unmistakable. The leaves are similar, and the glistening white, green-centered flowers are nearly identical, reduced in size but disproportionately large for the plant. From mid-August to mid-September you see it as pictured here, studded with pea-size berries of brilliant red. It deciduates for the winter, but what a joy it is for the remainder of the year.

Bunchberry thrives in northern gardens in acid soils that are moist and well-draining. In other sites it has a more difficult time, and we know of no other plant that will provide all the features of bunchberry. The snowdrop anemone (*Anemone sylvestris*) is about the same height and has a wild charm about it. It has no red berries, but its foliage and long-lasting white spring flowers are completely delightful. The driftwood, ferns, and shrubby backdrop in the example all contribute to the effect, and look-alikes are available for any garden in any climate.

Plate 84. Bunchberry in Acadia National Park, Maine.

A Scattering of Elderberry Blossoms on Flagstone

Flagstones set in gravel make a path to the corner of a cedar fence at one of our garden's entrances. It's a pleasant spot, but for most of the year not especially distinguished. Then, in late June, the neighbor's golden elderberry (*Sambucus canadensis* 'Aurea') begins to shed its blossoms, and for two weeks it rains one-quarter-inch white stars onto the rock (Plate 85). Every so often a breeze comes up and sweeps the rock clean, but within a few hours, the tiny firmament is renewed, and again it's a wonder, and again it's a delight. As completely reliable and welcome as it is, the effect was totally unplanned.

Ever since the first magical occurrence of this effect, we have done our best to prepare various corners of the garden to receive such fortuitous blessings: Johnny-jump-ups (*Viola tricolor*) were allowed to seed themselves into a gravel path, volunteer sapling aspen (*Populus tremuloides*) were encouraged to renew an aging grove, dark boulders were set to receive an autumn bounty of outrageously colorful maple leaves. True, these are transitory effects, short-lived pleasures that come and go in a matter of weeks, but when the main effects are gone, these little corners still have interest and provide a subtle backup for other sections of the garden. Every year, we look forward to a repeat of these small performances with as much excitement as the year before.

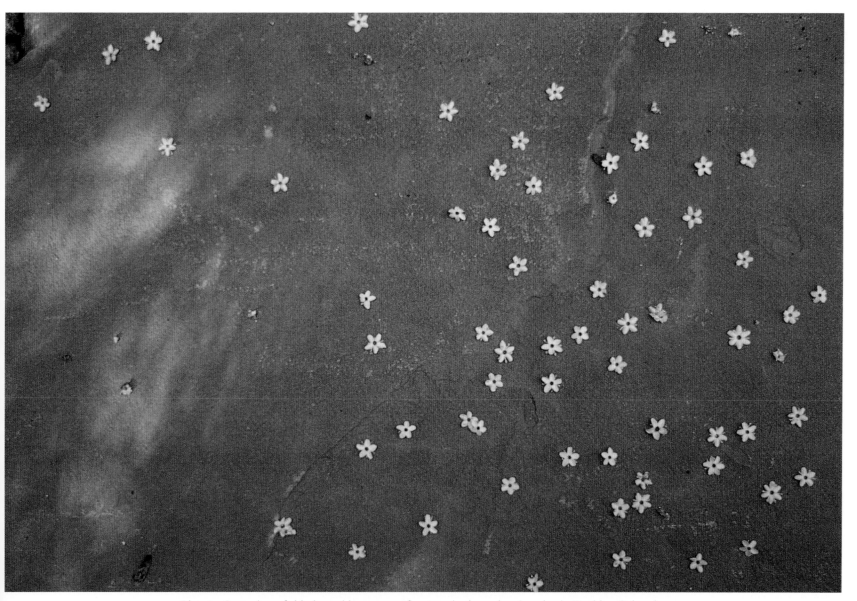

Plate 85. Scattering of elderberry blossoms on flagstone in the authors' garden in Boulder, Colorado.

Maple Leaves and Boulders

This is almost an autumn variation of our previous example, but in this case it is not blossoms that have rained down, but maple leaves, and the upright boulders are definitely not stepping stones (Plate 86). The leaves are painted in autumn's flashiest hues: red, yellow, orange, and a bit of summer's green thrown in for contrast. Although this small corner holds its own in every season, it is at its best in the fall. If the weather is cooperative, the display can linger for a glorious six weeks. Of course, many trees and shrubs boast spectacular fall color, but the maples, with their distinctively shaped leaves, may be the very best choice. Here in our Boulder, Colorado, garden, we used the Siberian maple (*Acer ginnala*). In warmer zones, say zones 6 through 9, one can choose from among the many superb small cultivars of Japanese maple (*A. palmatum*) or those of the fullmoon maple (*A. japonicum*). We can think of no better choices.

Of course, in design details such as these last two, it is impossible to plan the effect to the last detail; but this is what makes these kinds of effects so exciting and so different at every occurrence—a randomness, a spontaneity, a freshness that surprises us time after time.

Plate 86. Maple leaves and boulders in the authors' garden, Boulder, Colorado.

MOSS

Moss—billowy, velvety, and spongy soft—is the most luxuriant of all groundcovers. It is not to be walked on, however—it is too fragile for that kind of barbarism—and its strict cultural requirements strongly limit its use. Moss is a small-scale groundcover, one that can turn a corner of a garden into a very special place, a place rich with allusions to primitive forests.

In eastern Asia, moss plantings are cherished, and a famous garden in Kyoto is called simply The Moss Garden. Unfortunately, mosses have special needs, and most require deep shade, high humidity, and abundant water to thrive. Although these demands cannot always be met, there are many far more adaptable plants that can provide the same kind of effect. Of the four examples described here, two use real moss and two use a moss look-alike.

Golden Moss, Black Rock

Gold against black satin—that's how a jeweler might display the precious metal. Golden moss might be less precious, but it, too, is displayed to perfection when set off by a shiny black background. That is how we saw it along the Twin Falls Trail in Canada's Yoho National Park, growing atop of black schist slick with moisture (Plate 87). As with the display of a fine piece of jewelry, there is no clutter, and no superfluous embellishments to detract from the display; just the golden moss and the black rock—simple, restrained, and elegant—a jewel of a detail for the right garden setting.

Where heat, sunshine, or drought rule out the use of true moss, mosslike substitutes can be used to create a similar effect. Scotch moss (*Sagina subulata* 'Aurea') is not a true moss, but it is close enough in color and texture to be acceptable. Moreover, this pseudo-moss tolerates sun as well as light shade, and even a bit of foot traffic. It is hardy to zone 5 and maybe the gentler parts of zone 4. Another apt stand-in for golden moss is one of the vegetable sheep (*Raoulia lutescens*) of New Zealand. It, too, is evergreen (greener in the winter, much more golden in the summer), soft, billowing in habit, and very dense. Its growth is agonizingly slow, and an old patch may open up in the middle. For these reasons vegetable sheep is much more suitable for small areas than for large ones. For warmer climates (zone 8 and above), golden baby tears (*Soleirolia soleirolii* 'Aurea') can provide the look of moss with little of its trouble.

Plate 87. Golden moss against black rock along Twin Falls Trail in Yoho National Park, Canada.

Moss Garden on a Tropical Island

Half a world away, climbing La Soufrière on the island of Guadeloupe, we found a far different example (Plate 88). Here, rain and humidity are so abundant that moss is the predominant groundcover, carpeting acres of steep hillsides and the walls of deep canyons in a luxurious deep-pile mantle of gold. Yes, this moss is a tawny gold—lush, thick, undulating, and as soft to the touch as the finest fleece. Bromeliads and ferns add an occasional note of strong green to the composition, contrasting with the moss and complementing it.

This is a scene from a tropical isle, an exotic landscape with a special climate. Is there any hope of transferring it to more challenging climates? Absolutely! But only without using moss. Instead, one of the moss substitutes mentioned in the previous example can be used. Nor can bromeliads be used, except in the tropics, but there are a variety of alternatives. Some of the smaller forms of *Hosta* might be considered. Lily-turfs (*Liriope* and *Ophiopogon*) in the larger forms, with deep green leaves or black leaves, would provide sensational contrast. Maybe even a small-flowered, deep red daylily (*Hemerocallis*) could be used—or would this be too garish when in flower? Of course, a dark boulder here and there would set off the moss perfectly, providing contrast in texture as well as color. Play it as you will; a small corner of golden "moss" is likely to be a favorite highlight in the garden.

Plate 88. Moss garden on La Soufrière Trail, Guadeloupe.

The Mossy Look on a Grand Scale

Nowhere have we seen the serene beauty of moss better represented than in the exquisitely understated "moss" garden of the Hakone Japanese Garden in Saratoga, California (Plate 89). Perhaps the scale stretches the notion of detail a bit, but this example is so clearly stated and so magnificently successful that we had to include it.

The composition occupies a fairly flat, rectangular area and consists of nothing else but a mossy groundcover and a lone tree placed a bit off center. That is all there is to it—strikingly simple and strikingly beautiful. The tree, perhaps a flowering cherry, has been pruned to a slender framework. As the sun passes overhead, the shadow of the tree draws an ever-changing linear pattern across the moss. It's a subtle effect, but a great deal of time can be captured under its spell.

What plays the role of moss in this masterful design is Irish moss, the green cultivar of *Sagina subulata*, so such an effect is realizable in zone 5, or even the gentler parts of zone 4. Another choice that we have found quite satisfactory is *Sedum* 'Green Acre' or *Sedum* 'Green Acre Minus', both evergreen, sun tolerant, shade tolerant (to some degree), highly drought tolerant, and hardy in zone 3. The role of the tree could be played by almost any slender graceful tree of moderate size, not too leafy, not too dense. A clump of birch—paper birch (*Betula papyrifera*) or European white birch (*B. pendula*)—might be the best choice of all. Some shadblow (*Amelanchier*), *Stewartia*, or a Washington thorn (*Crataegus phaenopyrum*) might serve nearly as well. The look of moss may be the central feature, but it's the shadow play of the branches on the moss that gives this landscape its special magic.

Plate 89. The mossy look on a grand scale, at the Hakone Japanese Garden, Saratoga, California.

"Moss" in the Colorado Sun

The photo of the stone staircase in the authors' garden shows *Sedum* 'Green Acre' playing the role of moss on a dry hillside with a southwest exposure in Boulder, Colorado (Plate 90). The soil is a sandy bentonite clay: quick-drying, crusty, not in the least friable, and strongly alkaline. Actually, we seldom call it soil—"dirt" is how we refer to it when we want to be polite. Yet, the sedum is right at home; it does not fry in the sun, freeze to brown in the winter, or demand any more water than the paltry amount allotted annually by nature. We never fertilize it, never treat it for bugs or disease, and never mow it. Even so, it rewards us with this verdant, cushiony look of moss season after season, year after year. Only for a few weeks in June is the deception revealed, when the sedum covers itself with a mantle of tiny, shiny, yellow, star-shaped flowers.

Actually, the sedum does not need such austere conditions to survive. It will take a bit of shade and even some moisture when offered, although too much of either will cause the tight growth to open, making a shabby mess out of an otherwise neat plant. Another candidate for a mossy effect is rupturewort (*Herniaria glabra*)—horrible name for such a fine and useful plant. It tolerates and appreciates the same conditions as *Sedum* 'Green Acre', but its color is a much darker green, and its texture is not as soft. Other candidates to consider for the same conditions include short, tight-growing *Dianthus* like 'Tiny Rubies', any low-growing *Veronica*, and several of the low-growing thymes (*Thymus*). But for color or texture, none is as suitable a substitute for moss as *Sedum* 'Green Acre'.

Plate 90. *Sedum* playing the role of moss in the authors' garden, Boulder, Colorado.

Red Water, Green Sedge

Red water, green sedge—a startling and unlikely combination that we found along the Paint Pots Trail in Canada's Kootenay National Park (Plate 91). The land here is rich in iron oxide, a mineral used as a pigment by the native tribes of the area and mined earlier in this century for use as a paint pigment, and it is this substance that gives the sandy marshy soil its brownish red color. Few plants other than the sedge venture into the water. Maybe the concentration of iron oxide is too poisonous; maybe the fine-textured red soil is too densely compacted; maybe the pools fill and dry too erratically. Whatever the reason, the result is a spare, abstract landscape of striking contrasts.

To achieve this effect in a cultivated garden, one might cover the bottom of a system of shallow pools with a fine red sand, the kind sold by gravel suppliers for use in cement, soil mixes, and paths. The water itself could be tinted with a vegetable dye, as is so often done with lily pools. With the choice of coloring agent under the control of the designer, we would expect that the pools would provide an acceptable environment for many plants in addition to water-loving grasses and sedges. Iris such *Iris laevigata*, *I. pseudacorus*, Louisiana hybrids, and others with white or yellow flowers, buttercup (*Ranunculus*) of many kinds, and horsetails (*Equisetum*) might be appropriate. *Primula* would be too fancy, *Ligularia* too dandy, and big-leaved, bold species such as gunnera (*Gunnera manicata*), Japanese butterbur (*Petasites japonicus*), and umbrella plant (*Peltiphyllum peltatum*) too overpowering. The red water should

Plate 91. Red water and green sedge, Paint Pots Trail, Kootenay National Park, Canada.

not be hidden by the plants, for it is the main color component of this design against which all other elements are played. It is this component that distinguishes this singular landscape and makes it so memorable.

THE PRIMAL BEAUTY OF FERNS

Once the land was ruled by ferns. During the carboniferous period, 345–280 million years ago, vast regions of land supported forests of tree ferns that reached upward to 60 ft (18 m). Today the reign of tree ferns is restricted to only a few regions, and even where found, the colonies are seldom extensive. There are still some species that attain a height of 40 ft (12 m), but most ferns are of modest size. Ferns grow in a variety of different sites, in a variety of different soils, and in a variety of different climates, so it is not surprising to find them in a variety of different gardens around the world. Wherever ferns are found, they grace the landscape with their distinctive primitive beauty. Lacking flowers, it is their diverse forms and subtle colors that enchant the viewer, and their origins in the far distant past only adds to the fascination.

We have seen so many extraordinary examples of ferns in the landscape that it was difficult to choose among them. Here are a few of our favorites.

Golden Ferns

A display of color coming from that subtle and most low-key of plant clans, the ferns, is quite unexpected. But in Rocky Mountain National Park, along Fern Lake Trail, when autumn captures the highcountry, the bracken fern (*Pteridium aquilinum*) are Midas-touched by the chill and color to a golden-yellow hue. They are common along the trail, but uncommonly beautiful at this time of the year, especially when seen against a dark stream or carpeting a grove of aspen. Most dramatic of all is to see them set off against a dark boulder or, as we see here (Plate 92), against the black trunk of an ancient pine. The golden display can last for three weeks or only a few days, it's all up to the weather—fickle mountain weather at that. Cloaked in its autumn finery, bracken has its finest moment. This deciduous fern is also of interest in the spring, however, offering a vertical accent of furry crosiers; and the bright green fronds of summer are elegant enough to grace a florist's bouquet.

In the garden, a single fern displayed against a boulder or tree trunk creates a dramatic effect—the laciness of the fern contrasted against the hard contours of the rock or tree trunk. Many ferns thrive under cultivation and would fit nicely into such a design. The wood ferns (*Dryopteris*) are superb, and some have the advantage of being evergreen. Not so the autumn fern (*D. erythrosora*), which displays its autumn coloration of bronzy reds in the spring only. The Japanese painted fern (*Athyrium nipponicum* 'Pictum') is colorful for most of the year, but more subtly so. One could use interrupted fern (*Osmunda claytonia*), cinnamon fern (*O. cinnamonea*), lady fern (*Athyrium filix-femina*), hay-scented fern (*Dennstaedtia punctilobula*), and many others, although finding one that can compete with the bracken fern for fall color is not that easy. Of course, a small shrub like an azalea (*Rhododendron*) or a wild rose

Plate 92. Golden ferns, Fern Lake Trail, Rocky Mountain National Park, Colorado.

(*Rosa*), or some clump of perennial like shasta daisy (*Chrysanthemum maximum*), can be used in such a setting, but with a great loss of subtlety. There is something very special about ferns.

Fern and Birch in a Bronzed Landscape

A misty rain began to fall as we started our hike up to Lost Man Lake in Vermont's Smuggler's Notch State Park. The mist filtered the sunlight to a bronzy glow that plated both plants and stone with a metallic luster. All color was muted and all form flattened to a bas-relief. At the very beginning of the trail we came upon a stone alcove housing a young birch, a cluster of ferns, and a few other plants—a surreal arrangement of serene beauty (Plate 93).

Much of the effect of this composition depends on the dark stone alcove, but maybe a stone wall could provide the same sort of background, at least for color and texture. The other components of the design are easily provided. The birch, probably a gray birch (*Betula populifolia*), could be replaced by paper birch (*B. papyrifera*), or European white birch (*B. pendula*), or Japanese birch (*B. platyphylla* var. *japonica*), but with some loss of subtlety. Aspen (*Populus tremuloides*) might be considered, or even some *Stewartia*, but the latter are scene-stealers that might unbalance the overall design. For the fern component, we would choose from among the wood ferns (*Dryopteris*), a genus with several bold, shiny-leaved ferns that have the decided advantage of being evergreen. Of course, many deciduous ferns are visually just as well-suited, but what a pleasure to be able to enjoy such a landscape feature throughout the year.

Plate 93. Fern and birch in Smuggler's Notch State Park, Vermont.

Maidenhair Fern and Maple

The next example of using ferns in the landscape comes from our own backyard in Boulder, Colorado. A maidenhair fern (*Adiantum pedatum*) and a young Oregon vine maple (*Acer circinatum*) are tucked into the rocky bank of a small cascades that we constructed. It's a simple arrangement whose delicate beauty delights us with three full seasons of pleasure. Autumn makes it even more special, when the first frosts tint the fern auburn and splash the maple leaves with red and orange (Plate 94).

For airy grace, nothing can outdo the northern maidenhair fern (*Adiantum pedatum*), and it is hardy to zone 3. Other ferns can be considered but are unlikely to match this one in elegance and fall color. The fullmoon maple (*Acer japonicum*) is a look-alike replacement for the vine maple and will color as well. The Japanese maple (*A. palmatum*), with a different but equally superb leaf shape, also offers spectacular fall color and is available in several small-growing cultivars. For the truly frigid garden, say in zone 2, gardeners can opt for the Siberian maple (*A. ginnala*). Any of these reworkings should require next to no maintenance, and for the neglect will reward you with a spot of beauty year after year.

Plate 94. Maidenhair fern and maple in the authors' garden, Boulder, Colorado.

A Canyon of Ferns

The room that serves as the hub of a complex of greenhouses in the Brooklyn Botanic Garden in New York is designed to give the visitor a window into the subtropics. Glass walls surround the visitor on three sides, affording a panoramic view of what seems to be the rock wall of a canyon on which a variety of exotic plants are growing (Plate 95). Convincing though it may be, it is not real rock that forms the background but rather cast stone, cement cast in place and then modeled and colored to look like real rock, which it does most effectively. Banded with different colors—gray, black, tan—creased and folded into the contrapuntal rhythms that geological forces give to natural rock, the walls of this display can be viewed as dynamic sculpture, something of beauty and interest in itself. The plants featured are not grouped according to place of origin or even type or habitat, but rather by how well they fit into the setting. There are few rare plants and few that are difficult to grow. Imagine this display without the glass, and you have a rich set of themes for a garden wall.

Ferns and cycads play a major role in the design, and their shapes complement each other—a rosette of fronds or frond-shaped leaves, the entire form sessile or supported on a short trunk. These similarities lend a homogeneity to the design, although there are more than enough differences to sustain interest. In the section pictured in Plate 95, the small fern near the center is a rabbit's-foot fern (*Davallia* or *Humata*). The other plants in the photo are cycads: the sago palm (*Cycas revoluta*) with narrow leaflets, and the Jamaica sago tree (*Zamia furfuracea*) with oval leaflets having the texture of cardboard. Rabbit's-foot ferns are commonly available in a variety of similar species, but none are suitable for temperate gardens. However, the lady fern (*Athyrium filix-femina*) and others of the genus *Athyrium* or some of the wood ferns (*Dryopteris*) would make suitable substitutes in zones 3 through 7. Unfortunately, there are no cycads for temperate gardens, but ferns can make reasonable substitutes for these too. For this purpose, one needs something big and bold, say one of the *Osmunda* ferns such as cinnamon fern (*O. cinnamonea*) or interrupted fern (*O. claytonia*).

The rock wall can be pieced together using natural stone, or artificial stone cast in place, or a combination of both techniques. In either case, one can do no better than to follow the example at hand, providing some variety in color and rhythm in the surface of the rock. This is what gives the wall its dynamic character and gives it enough interest to enhance any garden on its own. The plants add yet another dimension of interest and beauty that we of course would not want to do without.

Plate 95. Fern on a canyon wall behind glass at the Brooklyn Botanic Garden, Brooklyn, New York.

Ferns and Vines at Riverside

Lost Man Creek in Redwood National Park, California, is more than wide enough to be called a river; certainly out of scale with anything one might consider as a garden detail. Throughout its course, however, the creek is fed by tributaries of modest size, and along the banks of these tributaries, one often finds a small, unexplored corner of extraordinary beauty.

Streamside Fernery

A bit off the path near the beginning of Lost Man Creek Trail, we found just such a tributary, and in a little inlet, even more secluded, we discovered a cove of ferns (Plate 96). Abundant rainfall, Pacific mists, and the shade of giant trees all combine to make this fern heaven. Ferns are the predominant groundcover in this region, and in the cove they were growing to perfection. Many genera of ferns are represented, including maidenhair fern (*Adiantum*), lady fern (*Athyrium*), brittle fern (*Cystopteris*), wood fern (*Dryopteris*), and sword fern (*Polystichum*). One can also see mosses, sedges, and a variety of other plants.

We cannot imagine a more apt choice of plants to grace a small pond or stream, nor a planting that is easier to establish and easier to maintain. There are so many ferns for so many climates that this design can be realized almost anywhere, from the far North to the far South. The effect is robust enough to hold up under all sorts of variations without diminishing it—a perfect treasure for almost any garden.

Plate 96. Streamside fernery along Lost Man Creek, Redwood National Park, California.

A Vine Rambles Over a Fallen Redwood

Near the cove of ferns, we found another delightful spot, this scene composed of only two elements: a fallen redwood and a coastal manroot vine or western wild cucumber (*Marah oreganus*) (Plate 97). The weatherworn, reddish log not only gave support to the meandering vine but also set off the bold, brilliant green, shiny leaves to perfection. A spot garden—a niche of simple, compelling beauty—a bit of design easily transferred to a cultivated landscape.

Of course, the fallen log need not be redwood, and we would not be ashamed to use a bit of redwood stain in order to achieve the contrast in color that is so striking in nature's example at Lost Man Creek. The vine could be any of many rangy, bold-leaved cultivars of Balkan or English ivy (*Hedera helix*), or Virginia creeper (*Parthenocissus quinquefolia*), or Boston ivy (*P. tricuspidata*). Choose the right cultivar and either Virginia creeper or Boston ivy will end the season with a blaze of incandescent color: yellow, purple, or red—your choice. And what else would be needed? Not a thing.

Plate 97. Cucumber vine on fallen redwood, Lost Man Creek, Redwood National Park, California.

DESIGN WITH A TWIST

Pruning and shaping trees and shrubs is a fine art akin to sculpture; and as with sculpture, there are good examples of pruning and there are bad examples. There are fine pieces of bonsai, dwarfed and sculpted trees that evoke the most noble and moving trees seen in the wild, and there are preposterous examples of topiary that evoke images of Bugs Bunny and Mickey Mouse. Wielding a manual hedge-clipper is enough to try one's restraint, but with the out-and-out power of electric clippers and pruning saws, the temptation to go from classical to baroque to rococo to bizarre to grotesque is nearly irresistible.

Even nature at times seems to veer toward the rococo and beyond. But usually the result is not only acceptable, but downright fascinating, and we are led to reconsider and expand our notion of natural form. We have in mind two examples of wondrously shaped trees, one found in the wild and the other in a city garden; in each case the shaping was done by nature's hand alone.

Wind Espalier

Our first example is found in Acadia National Park in Maine, near Otter Point (Plate 98). Espaliered flat against a granite cliff is a spruce (*Picea*), sheared and pruned to a shape reminiscent of Chinese calligraphy. The tools that nature used here to sculpt this extraordinary form are the gale winds that so often come in from the Atlantic Ocean and crash against this seaside rampart.

Although some may see this form as too strange, too unnatural, too contrived, we see it as simply wonderful, far more satisfying than any piece of espalier that we have seen from human hands. We see no reason why such artistry cannot be applied in a cultivated garden in a restricted space to create a striking backdrop against a building or a wall. Of course, it takes some time and effort to get such a project started, and more time and effort to bring it to mature form, but even the initial stages will be fascinating.

Plate 98. Wind espalier, Coast Trail, Acadia National Park, Maine.

A Different Twist

Our second example of naturally sculpted trees is taken from Golden Gate Park in San Francisco, California. Here we found a grove of New Zealand tea trees (*Leptospermum*), as bizarrely beautiful a bunch of bent timber as one can imagine (Plate 99). Even the eighteenth-century Japanese masters of the silk screen could not devise more fanciful forms. Even ignoring shape, the trunks themselves are works of art—dark, rough textured, and ribbed like thick cords twisted together to make giant ropes. The serpentine trunk and branches weave this way and that, seldom reaching upward, often doubling back on themselves with a logic to the growth pattern that is entirely their own.

Leptospermum are fine-leaved evergreens that bear a profusion of small red, pink, or white blossoms for many weeks in the spring and summer, blossoms that remind us of those of alpine saxifrages. Although we have never seen this grove in flower, the effect must be sensational. They are trees for warmer regions, zone 9 and above, and we know of no trees for harsher climates that offer such a wonderfully peculiar pattern of growth. Several small shrubby oaks, like Rocky Mountain white oak (*Quercus gambelii*) and bear oak (*Q. ilicifolia*), have a tendency to twist in strange ways, seemingly lost in their quest for sunlight; maybe the artful gardener can further encourage this misdirection to get an approximation of the tea trees. Wisterias, particularly *Wisteria floribunda* and *W. sinensis*, can be coaxed into assuming self-supporting tree shapes and when mature develop a thick trunk and limbs with the look of twisted rope. And when wisteria flowers, no tree or vine can surpass it, not even New Zealand tea tree.

Unlike most of the landscape effects that we describe, a long time is needed to sculpt a tree or vine into forms like those in this example. But this grove of *Leptospermum* is so distinctive and so fascinating that we had to include it. Maybe there is a quick and easy way to get this effect, but we doubt it.

Plate 99. A different twist from Golden Gate Park, San Francisco, California.

Wildflowers in a Mountain Meadow

One expects a mountain meadow to offer a bounty of wildflowers, and Beaver Meadows in Colorado's Rocky Mountain National Park does just that every summer. Walk through this meadow in July and you will be surrounded by color—not a sea of color, but points, spots, and splashes of it here and there. Still, it's a bit overwhelming, and it can be difficult to focus your attention on the details. But there are always small features to be found that are distinctive enough to hold their own even in such grand surroundings.

A spot containing a gathering of wildflowers around a granite boulder is just such a simple but striking arrangement (Plate 100). Growing together in a surprisingly small area we found Indian paintbrush (*Castilleja*), wall flower (*Erysimum*), pearly everlasting (*Anaphalis*), buttercup (*Ranunculus*), and several other species, enjoying the protection offered by the boulder. Seldom does one find in nature such a concentration of different plants in such a small area, but this is exactly what many gardeners strive for—an assortment of plants that will provide a harmonious but varied flower show for many months. What more effective way is there to maintain interest in the garden?

Translating this bit of flowery meadow to a garden presents no problems whatsoever. Many of the plants seen in the example are readily available and quite adaptable. Substitutions to fit your individual tastes are also easy to find and too numerous to mention.

Although this might not be the most novel of features, its long period of bloom is likely to make it a favorite spot from late spring to early fall.

A Residential Subalpine Meadow

Our neighbors have a small, flower-filled island garden in their front yard (Plate 101). The garden features a mix of annuals and perennials, some striking pieces of driftwood, and nothing else. It's the kind of scene that one might find in a subalpine meadow, although the mix of plants is considerably more diverse and flamboyant than what one is likely to meet in the wild.

Careful attention was given to colors and form to provide variety while maintaining the coherence of the design, a delicate balancing act so well planned that the garden is a delight from whatever angle you choose to view it—and the view of it from any angle is an invitation to see it from all other angles. The choice of plants has been so skillfully made that the garden is awash in bloom from early spring to late fall, yet changes dramatically from month to month as colors and forms come and go. The owners accomplished this using only plants that are readily available: Asiatic lilies (*Lilium*), chrysanthemums (*Chrysanthemum*), purple coneflower (*Echinacea purpurea*), brown-eyed Susan (*Rudbeckia fulgida*), and many annuals. As small a feature as it is, it's an attention-getter, and few visitors pass by without taking notice.

No one should encounter any problem in re-creating this effect

Plate 100. Wildflowers in Beaver Meadows, Rocky Mountain National Park, Colorado.

in their own garden, whatever the climate; the only difficulty is maintaining some order and balance. Unrestrained enthusiasm abetted by a love of flowers can easily lead to a hodgepodge of elements. As always, a bit of restraint is in order, even in this design where variety and flamboyance is a keynote.

"To see the world in a grain of sand"—William Blake

"The large within the small" is one of the guiding principles of Japanese landscape design. The principle recommends the use of garden details that suggest grander themes and far larger landscapes. A raked bed of gravel may represent a stream, a lake, or even an expanse of ocean. Boulders may be placed to suggest mountains or islands. Three stones grouped together in a prescribed arrangement may be used to symbolize the sky, the earth, and humanity. Always, the representation is abstract enough to avoid the miniature-railroad effect of a slavishly literal downsizing of forms that involves no creativity and leaves nothing to the imagination.

Our example from the wild was taken from near a grand alpine lake, within a few hundred paces of Chasm Lake, at an altitude of nearly 12,000 ft (3,600 m) in Rocky Mountain National Park. After the snow finally yields to the warmth of summer in late June, for a brief few months water stands in pools barely larger than a bathtub, or runs freely in small streams. Here we have an example of a pint-size pool that suggests the larger landscape of which it is a part (Plate 102).

The pool, maybe 6 ft (1.8 m) across at its widest dimension, is

Plate 101. Residential subalpine meadow, Boulder, Colorado.

Plate 102. Miniature lake, Chasm Lake Trail, Rocky Mountain National Park, Colorado.

backed by boulders less than 2 ft (0.6 m) high. But squint to see only it, ignoring the panoramic view of the surrounding Rockies, and it becomes a vast lake above which towers a grand range of mountains. Everything is in proportion, and the rhythm of the rock is the rhythm of the surrounding mountains. Even the reflection in the pool of the stone and the clouds heighten the illusion of a lake backed by massifs on a grand scale. Yet, the lack of inessential details avoids the miniature-railroad look completely. The allusions to the larger landscape are mostly a matter of imaginative interpretation, and that is what makes the scene so engaging.

A Gentle Cascades

Three massive slabs of rock, each with a shallow basin carved into its surface, are staggered stepwise down a gentle slope. From a source hidden in the shrubbery, a small stream of water is directed through sections of bamboo canes from one basin to the next until it spreads out to vanishing thinness over a bed of black river pebbles (Plate 103).

This small feature is part of the Japanese garden in the Denver Botanic Gardens in Denver, Colorado. The masterful design successfully incorporates both naturalistic and abstract elements—not an easy feat. The various elements are joined together with a sure-handed conviction that reflects the clarity of intent, the skill, and the experience of the designer. Aspects of Japanese landscape style are employed in the arrangement, but such a feature would not be at all out of place in a naturalistic design without any other orien-

tal overtones. And what a delightful feature it would be in some secluded corner of a private garden! The geometry of the design and the play of water over the rocks would make it a favorite spot.

Of course, the stone basins on which the composition is focused are rather special. Such shapes are not easy to find, not easy to transport even if you should be lucky enough to find them, and not easy to set in place. The obvious alternative is to use artificial stone, cement cast in place. Sculpting the stone to stack properly and to catch and transport water is neither difficult nor expensive—especially when weighed against the effect that will be created.

Ice Plants for the North

Ice plants were thought to be adapted only to gardens in zone 8 and warmer climates. After all, these African succulents never experience a true winter in their native land—no snow, no ice, no week-long highs of subzero temperatures. Then gardeners found that several species of *Delosperma* will not only survive in zone 4, but thrive there with nearly weedy enthusiasm. Those used to seeing ice plants by the acre in the Southwest might laugh at our excitement over growing an ice plant in Boulder, Colorado, but here they are still something of a novelty, and we can still appreciate their beauty.

And what beauty it is, as we see in Plate 104, showing a patch of *Delosperma nubigenum* spilling over a low barrier of stone onto a path in the authors' garden. The time is late spring, and the radiant yellow blooms have been coming for weeks and will continue

Plate 103. Gentle cascades, Denver Botanic Gardens, Denver, Colorado.

coming for several more weeks. It's a carpet of pure sunshine that delights all who see it. When the blossoms fade, they leave hardly a trace, and the planting becomes a bright yellow-green, dense enough to suppress weeds and low enough to require no maintenance. So small are the fat leaves (about 0.5 in [1.3 cm]) that the plant gives the effect of a coarse moss, at least if you stand back a bit and squint. When the chill of autumn works its magic, the entire planting is repainted, first in gold, then in bronze, and finally in a clear and shining red that lasts throughout the winter and into spring. What an exciting display of color it makes when the snow begins to retreat!

The only problem with using *Delosperma* or other ice plants as a little feature is that they have an irrepressible drive to grow into a really big feature. *Delosperma* never bullies larger plants or seeds itself about, however; instead, it tries to increase its hegemony by creeping along the ground and weakly rooting here and there. We wouldn't dare place it in a rockgarden near miniature alpine plants, but elsewhere as a groundcover it's easy to control. A gentle tug dislodges it in mats, and the pieces can be redeployed or discarded —not much of a chore, considering its spectacular yearlong contribution to the garden.

Other delospermas have been tried in zone 4 with varying success. *Delosperma ashtonii* and *D. lineare*, both with pink blossoms, are refined enough in habit and tame enough in growth to be trusted among alpine plants in the rockgarden. *Delosperma cooperi* is looser in habit than *D. nubigenum* and spreads even more rapidly, but it sets shocking fuchsia 2-in (5-cm) blossoms throughout the

Plate 104. Ice plant in the authors' garden in Boulder, Colorado.

224

summer. New ice plants are being introduced into temperate gardens each year, and some will no doubt make their way onto the list of the choicest groundcovers.

Many other succulents can be used for a spot of color in a natural setting: *Crassula*, *Rosularia*, *Sedum*, and *Sempervivum*, to name just a few. Special as they are, none put on a display that outshines that of the delospermas.

A Macramé of Sedum

It's the trees that draw visitors to Redwood National Park in California—redwoods, the world's tallest trees, towering to more than 350 ft (48 m) at maturity—but the park has other attractions besides the grand forests. The park extends to the shore of the Pacific Ocean, where one can walk the expansive beaches and explore the tide pools. We were doing just that when we came upon the base of a cliff accessible only at low tide. Colonies of Tinker-Toy-chained sedum (*Sedum spathulifolium*) clinging to the sheer face of black rock formed a wall-hanging of silver macramé (Plate 105)—a striking composition of contrasting color and form.

The range of this sedum is not restricted to the coast; it can be found inland in several states well away from the ocean. There are also other plants that can weave a silver pattern on a rock wall, plants that are much hardier and more adaptable, including other sedums as well as *Androsace*, *Saxifraga*, and *Sempervivum*. Not that these will yield exactly the same effect, but they can give a respectable approximation.

Plate 105. Macramé of sedum, Redwood National Park, California.

The main point that nature provides with this example is that a very small feature can have an extraordinarily big effect, an impact entirely out of proportion to its size, even when surrounded by a vast and magnificent landscape. So, in a garden, an area no more than a foot or so in diameter can hold some treasure that will bring you joy far exceeding its size.

Aspen and Brown-Eyed Susan

We have enjoyed this example of a landscape detail for nearly twenty years, for this is a small part of our own garden in Boulder (Plate 106). The design has two main elements: aspen (*Populus tremuloides*) and brown-eyed Susan (*Rudbeckia fulgida*) in the incomparable cultivar 'Goldsturm'.

Faithfully each year, for nearly two months from early August to late September, 'Goldsturm' lives up to its name, setting a golden storm of long-stemmed, brown-centered yellow-orange daisies against the smooth white trunks of the aspen. Even after petal fall, the rudbeckia is a delight: the prickly cones atop straight stems provide an ornament well into winter. Even the bold leaves please us, but since they emerge rather late in the season, we have interplanted near-species tulips of several kinds with the rudbeckia. The tulips provide a welcome splash of color in early spring, and when their leaves ripen and fade, the bold leaves of the rudbeckia make their appearance. The only other major component of the composition is a high groundcover of creeping grapeholly (*Mahonia repens*), one of our favorite broadleaf evergreens. The entire planting is a 6-ft (1.8-m) wide peninsula that protrudes about 10 ft (3 m) into the lawn from the perimeter of the shrub border. It can be seen from the patio deck and from the kitchen window, as well as from several different angles in the garden. When the brown-eyed Susans are in bloom, nothing else commands as much attention or gives us more pleasure.

As you see it, the planting is suitable for zones 3 through 6, although the aspen will be none too happy in the warmer zones. Birch (*Betula*) or maybe shadblow (*Amelanchier*) might be better choices in zones 5 through 7. As for a rudbeckia substitute, all sorts of pleasant daisies can be used, such as purple coneflower (*Echinacea purpurea*) in white or pink, shasta daisy (*Chrysanthemum maximum*), or various other single daisies. The rudbeckia is hardy from zone 3 to zone 10, however, and is surprisingly shade tolerant, making it as good a choice as any.

This entire arrangement requires little care, and through the years it has continued to reward us out of all proportion to the time, effort, and expense put into it. Come midsummer, it is the first place we go when walking in the garden.

Plate 106. Aspen and brown-eyed Susan in the authors' garden, Boulder, Colorado.

Plate 107. Stone lantern, Asticou Azalea Garden, Mount Desert Island, Maine.

Chapter 8

THE JAPANESE GARDEN

ROM the serene lakes and meadows of the lowlands to the windswept reaches of the alpine tundra, every landscape that we visited finds expression in some Japanese style garden. The tradition of the Japanese garden, unbroken for a thousand years, rests on the interpretation of nature, idealized, formalized, and presented with a clarity that can only come from a profound sensitivity to the wonder and beauty of the world around us.

What is it that gives these gardens their unique character? Surely it's more than just a stone lantern and a water basin. As in all of Japanese art, these gardens show a distinctive penchant for simplicity and refined understatement. Extraordinary attention is paid to detail and composition. Each plant, each stone, each water feature is given its due, both as a point of interest to be enjoyed in its own right and as a component in the overall design. Grand themes are implied by humble materials and are never overstated. Gravel is raked into wave forms to suggest moving water, a stream or even an ocean lapping at a beach; trees are bent and pruned to the heroic shapes of those found in the alpine regions. Common plants are carefully placed and meticulously maintained to display their simple beauty, a beauty that familiarity might otherwise mask.

Almost always, one sees in these gardens a balance between formal elements and free-form elements, between creative abstraction and faithful interpretation. A precisely arched bridge might span a meandering stream; gravel carefully raked into concentric circles might set off free-form boulders; a straight path of rectangular stones might lead to a grove of wind-sculpted trees transplanted from the highlands. Modern design trends in Japanese gardens further challenge our precepts of naturalistic design: huge boulders are partly carved and polished; trees are sculpted and cast in aluminum; and concrete is used freely to create bridges, walks, and benches. This general principle of contrast is present in virtually all Japanese garden styles and may be the main characteristic that they share in common. It is a stylistic device that at once defines the garden as a human enterprise distinct from nature's works and pays homage to nature's designs. In all their variety, these are garden styles of the utmost elegance, serene and controlled.

The Japanese-style garden has its detractors, however. Some

westerners criticize these gardens as being too formal, abstract to the point of appearing contrived. They see the finely tonsured plants, precisely manicured mosses, and perfectly raked gravel as anything but naturalistic. Moreover, they believe that anything short of perfection will detract from the garden's effect, and so they fear that any adaptation of these design principles will doom the owner of such a garden to yearlong slavery in pursuit of perfect neatness. But there are elements of the Japanese style that do just the opposite, elements that lead to a relatively carefree and inexpensively maintained garden. For example, paths are made of stone and gravel, and groundcover plants are used that require no mowing. This is a much more sensible approach than planting vast areas in the bluegrass that plagues so many of our gardens and usurps our weekends. Pruning chores can be kept under control by using plants that are genetic dwarfs. For example, clones of pines and maples are available that mature at a fraction of their species' height. The sense of harmony so evident in the Japanese garden is partly due to a restrained use of plants—few varieties are grown, and the plants are seldom crowded—another factor that keeps care at a reasonable level.

In this tradeoff for control over unbridled exuberance, the Japanese styles often yield gardens of more subtle interest, more deeply evocative of nature's themes, more restful and contemplative. Abstraction and simplicity do not allow an easy escape from mediocre composition, and a lack of inspiration cannot be masked by a hodgepodge of plants or ersatz garden ornaments. Abstrac-

tion and simplicity can, however, reveal the essential beauty and nobility of a landscape. So for those who most admire gardens that evoke the wonder and beauty of nature, for those who see the best of garden design as the creative reworking of themes from nature, the Japanese garden styles represent the ultimate expression of the art of landscape design.

Asticou Azalea Garden

Tucked into the far northeast corner of the United States, off the coast of Maine, is Mount Desert Island. About 60 percent of the island is occupied by Acadia National Park, and most of the remaining land is privately owned; but a small state-owned garden shares a piece of the park's northeast boundary. Asticou Azalea Garden was given to the state of Maine as a public park by Nelson Rockefeller. A bit out of the way for most visitors to the national park and to mainland Maine, it receives only a small fraction of the attention it deserves. All the better for those who do visit, for this is a garden that one should enjoy in as much privacy as possible.

The garden is comprised of several smaller gardens, each representing a different style. There is a dry landscape, a small rockgarden, a good-size lake, and an intimate pool, each with a distinctive character of its own. The pieces fit together perfectly to make a varied landscape evoking many moods. Three of our favorite sections are pictured in Plates 107–109. Plate 107 shows a well-weathered stone lantern peeking out from behind a richly textured tree trunk.

Plate 108. Bridge, Asticou Azalea Garden, Mount Desert Island, Maine.

There is a pixyish aspect about the lantern that some might find a bit cloying, but we find it delightful and just a bit amusing.

Close by, a bridge arches across a stream (Plate 108). Powerful but graceful, carved out of a single slab of granite, the bridge has a gentle arch that contradicts its weight and complements the curves of the stream. Plants are used with restraint and do not compete for attention. Harmony is the vehicle that establishes the mood of serenity throughout the garden.

Near the bridge and just off the path is a pool (Plate 109). The ancient trees and the woodland understory communicate a much greater sense of privacy and seclusion here. The trees that you see in the photo are birches—a river birch (*Betula nigra*) and a paper birch (*B. papyrifera*)—their differences disguised under the rough bark of old age. Azaleas, hostas, and ferns are carefully positioned about the trees to create a naturalistic but clearly idealized understory planting. When we arrived, a cool mist had settled onto the scene, and it was gently raining. Monet would have been delighted.

Asticou Azalea Garden is located in a cold zone 4, and winter can be counted on to bring heavy snow, numbing cold, and icy gales from the Atlantic. On the other hand, summer can be hot and humid. So the hardiness of the plants used here cannot be questioned, at least where there is adequate snow cover. Azaleas and other ericaceous shrubs play a major role in the design. In a drier climate and on alkaline soils, this model has to be modified. *Viburnum* of many kinds, bush cinquefoil (*Potentilla fruticosa*), *Spiraea*, *Daphne*, chokeberry (*Aronia*), and many kinds of dwarf almond, cherry, and other *Prunus* could be used. Grapehollies (*Mahonia*), boxwood (*Buxus*), various true hollies (*Ilex*), and dwarf conifers would be effective during the winter months. It is the overall structure of the design that determines its great appeal, however, and not the particular plants that are used—an important principle illustrated by natural landscapes and naturalistic gardens over and over again.

Plate 109. Pool and birch, Asticou Azalea Garden, Mount Desert Island, Maine.

Japanese Garden in Stanley Park

Westfield, Massachusetts, is a small upscale town of fewer than forty-thousand people. You might think it barely large enough to support Saturday night bingo games at the town hall. In fact, the town boasts a 200-acre park, Stanley Park, which features recreational fields, a 5-acre arboretum, and a magnificent Japanese garden.

Near one of the entrances to the Japanese garden is a small pavilion that provides shelter from sun or rain while offering a superb view (Plate 110). A gazebo in a European garden would do the same, but the design of this structure is pure Japanese—understated and with no hint of ostentation. The strong simple lines of the structure set off the gentle curves of the path, and the dark brown color of the wood is a perfect foil for the plants. There can be no more effective backdrop for the bed of sunny daffodils, or for the crabapple when it is wreathed in a cloud of white bloom. Even the more modestly colored plants play well against it.

After the crabapple and the daffodils finish their great show, the golden juniper (*Juniperus*) and burgundy barberry (*Berberis*) continue to contribute color throughout the year. Perhaps for the purist they add too much color, or color that is too flamboyant, or maybe too harsh. Perhaps they see these shrubs as obscuring the contemplative and serene mood of the garden, the attribute that most people consider the very soul of the Japanese style. These crit-

ics may have a point, but who can deny that this garden is strikingly beautiful and that it gains in excitement and originality what a more traditional approach would miss. Of course, replacing the highly colored juniper and barberry with cultivars of tamer hues would emphasize the more traditional character of the design.

The path is simple and traditional—flagstones set in gravel— visually satisfying and virtually carefree. As far as maintenance is concerned, this is a much more sensible approach than that usually taken in the West, where gravel is often reserved as a groundcover for island plantings and grass is used for walkways. Nor do the plants require much maintenance; most of those used are hardy, pest free, and slow growing. Juniper and barberry need only an occasional grooming, and the trees may need a bit of pruning every other year.

This garden includes no large trees, and the plants are not crowded. The garden was planned that way, and it is not merely a reflection of its youth. The result is a sun-filled design, open and spacious, that seems to create more space than it occupies. The whole effect is more lighthearted than the usual interpretations of the Japanese aesthetic, albeit perhaps not as restful or contemplative. But for current tastes, just such an adaptation may be the most satisfying of all.

Plate 110. Japanese garden in Stanley Park, Westfield, Massachusetts.

Japan as Seen in Brooklyn

Japanese garden splendor in Brooklyn, New York—implausible perhaps, but that is exactly what the Brooklyn Botanic Garden offers (Plate III). Park your car, walk past the entrance booth and the small planting of antique roses, and soon you reach a gate— your entrance to another culture and another time. A few steps through the gate and you find yourself in a pavilion overlooking a serene lake, the centerpiece of the garden. Overhead, a lath trellis supports a tangle of wisteria vines. In May, the vines drape panicles of pale lilac blossoms through the slats, and a sweet fragrance gently envelops the pavilion. You can happily spend your entire visit right here, looking out over the lake and the surrounding gardens, and come away feeling that your time was well-spent. To enjoy the design to the fullest, however, you need to walk around the shore, for hidden corners offer treasures that are barely hinted at when viewed from the pavilion.

Among the first of many grand views is across the long axis of the lake. In the marshy margins of the foreground, an expanse of *Iris pseudacorus* displays its rushlike foliage and brilliant yellow blossoms against the water. Further along the path, a group of weeping cherry trees (*Prunus subhirtella* var. *pendula*) lean over the lake, their branch tips barely above the surface. They bloom in April, erupting in clouds of pale pink. Although superb from any viewpoint, this grove when in flower is particularly stunning from the pavilion, from where you can see the pink reflected in the blue water.

Walking past the cherry trees, you come upon the section pictured in Plate III, a section small enough to be part of a private garden. Its design is distinctly Japanese—you would think so even without the customary trappings: the arched bridge, the red-lacquered torii standing in the water, and the traditional plant material. Soft billowing, flowing masses of foliage border the bridge, one side embraced by the burgundy foliage of a dwarf weeping Japanese maple (*Acer palmatum*), the other by an undulating mound of white-flowered wisteria (*Wisteria floribunda*). Ferns enjoy the damp soil at the lake's edge. In the distance, we see the stand of yellow flag iris (*Iris pseudacorus*) that we encountered at the beginning of the path. From this view, the lake seems more like a pond, the scale perfect for a private garden of even modest size.

The plants used here are widely adaptable, from the warmer parts of zone 4 through most of zone 7, and the iris and ferns will take zone 3 without complaint. Those needing plants of even greater cold hardiness can substitute some dwarf variety of Siberian maple (*Acer ginnala*) for the Japanese maple, but we know of no cultivar that will give you the burgundy color or weeping habit. The wisteria can be replaced by silver lace vine (*Polygonum aubertii*) or maybe some *Clematis*, neither choice presenting as interesting a foliage mass. Other replacements come to mind, but none equal the casual grace of the Japanese maple and the wisteria.

Plate III. Japanese garden in the Brooklyn Botanic Garden, Brooklyn, New York.

Postcard from Japan

One of the great lessons of the Japanese landscape masters is that bigger is not always better. Bonsai and saikei set the standard for landscapes small enough to be contained in trays or pots; tea garden designs brought the landscape to human size but in very restricted sites. Even the renowned stone gardens, so monumental when isolated in photographs, are often startlingly small. The great Zen Buddhist stone garden Ryoan-ji in Kyoto consists of nothing more than fifteen boulders in a bed of raked sand, the tallest stone in the garden barely waist high. Nevertheless, the viewer who is able to focus on the composition alone will see a mountain range rising out of the ocean.

For today's postcard-size suburban lots, smallness might not be a choice but rather a necessity. To honor this constraint, one can find no garden models more relevant than those from Japan. But smallness itself brings benefits that go beyond mere necessity. The small landscape is usually easy to maintain and easy to alter. The small landscape also offers an intimacy that cannot be achieved in a large-scale design. All of this makes the small Japanese-style garden a perfect choice to grace the grounds of a private residence. Our example here is just this sort of garden (Plates 112 and 113).

In the front yard of the Fleishman residence in West Hartford, Connecticut, a Japanese-style garden was designed on a plot no larger than 15 ft by 12 ft (4.5 m by 3.7 m). Within this small area, a landscape was created that offers variety and beauty far exceeding its modest size. There are dry rivulets laid out in gravel. Boulder arrangements set off ferns and iris. European ginger (*Asarum europaeum*) and mosses serve as groundcovers. The only woody plant is a dwarf crabapple (*Malus*) of some cultivar unknown to us, superbly pruned and meticulously maintained. So perfectly designed is this garden that it is a joy from every point of view: seeing it as you approach the house; as you view it from the living room within the house; and as you walk through it to examine the individual sections in detail.

Although the design is entirely coherent, strolling along the dry rivulets one can find a variety of vignettes of such beauty and interest that each is worthy of being viewed in isolation. These are the features that give interest to the garden throughout the season. There are so many details to enjoy that it easy to forget how small this garden is.

Most of the plants used in the garden are readily available from zone 3 through zone 7, and finding alternatives that will extend the range is not a problem. This design is suitable for many sites and many climates. No matter where such a garden is established, it is sure to bring its owners endless pleasure.

Plate 112. Private Japanese garden, Fleishman residence, West Hartford, Connecticut.

Plate 113. Another view of the Fleishman garden, West Hartford, Connecticut.

A National Treasure

The oriental arts are well-represented at the U.S. National Arboretum in Washington, D.C. The bonsai collection, its nucleus of ancient specimens a gift from the Japanese government, is considered to be one of the finest in the world. There is also a small but choice collection of tray landscapes (saikei and penjing). In autumn, the arboretum mounts a spectacular display of chrysanthemums trained in the cascade style; small, painstakingly pruned potted azaleas in extravagant full bloom take center stage in early spring.

The arboretum has two Japanese-style gardens. They are very different, and each is extraordinary. A traditional wooden gate provides entrance to one of them: a narrow, walled garden. On each side of the path, giant cryptomeria (*Cryptomeria japonica*), relatives of the redwoods, tower above the garden. Ferns, rare relatives of our Jack-in-the-pulpit (*Arisaema*), and unusual *Hosta* thrive in the deep shade beneath the trees. A rich, delicious scent arises from the forest floor and adds to the aura of antiquity and timelessness. We found this garden profoundly moving, serene and controlled in its understatement, and we walked through it again and again in rapt silence. As a model for a design to be realized in a dozen years or so, however, it is irrelevant. And the mood, so deeply affecting, may be considered by many to be more suitable for a religious retreat, rather than a secular garden.

By contrast, the other Japanese-style garden at the arboretum evokes a much different mood (Plate 114). Here the effect is more joyful than somber, more outgoing than introspective, and una-bashedly more decorative. The plants used in this garden are relatively fast growing and make a contribution well before maturity. The design is far more responsive to the seasons, and it is filled with light and color.

This garden is never more exuberant than in early spring, as shown in Plate 114. It is then that the azaleas are in full bloom. They cover the hillsides that border the path with billowing masses of color. Judging by those plants we saw that had flowered and those still in bud, the spectacle must go on for the better part of two months. Fern, bamboo, and hosta tone-down the picture a bit while adding variety and interest.

The flowering cherries (*Prunus serrulata*, *P. subhirtella*, and *P. ×yedoensis*) had already bloomed when we visited the garden, although their angular shape and glistening reddish brown bark make a contribution to the design throughout the year. A small grove of crapemyrtle (*Lagerstroemia indica*) is planted in front of one of the walls. Their time of full glory comes in summer when they cover themselves with pink and white panicles of blossoms. At other times, the richly marbled bark and the graceful pattern that these multi-stemmed, bushy trees make against the wall is enough of a contribution. (The National Arboretum is a center for the development of new crapemyrtles, and elsewhere in the arboretum there are fields of hybrids undergoing evaluation.) Still later in the season, the *Stewartia* will shine. They, too, have a magnificent bark pattern—a patchwork quilt of cream, tan, and gray—that makes them a treat at all times. The stewartias flower in late summer and early autumn with exquisite 2- to 3-in (5- to 7.5-cm) blooms like single, white camellias. Their foliage turns a coppery red at this time, and a more striking display is hard to imagine. Of course, Japanese maples (*Acer palmatum*) add yellow, red, and orange leaf color to the autumn scene, and they also contribute form and texture throughout the year.

You might argue that this garden's flamboyant use of color and diverse plant forms violate the Japanese tradition. Restraint, after all, is a hallmark of the Japanese aesthetic, and you might say that this garden is far too joyful, too boisterous, too hedonistic to be a fair representation. But you have to voice these reservations from afar, because when you are in its presence, the beauty of this garden will overwhelm all such criticisms.

What are the climate restrictions for such a garden? The planting as you see it is well-suited to zones 6 and 7, provided that the soil is acidic and has proper drainage and that the humidity is adequate. If you want to push this kind of garden inland or northward, some substitutions will have to be made. Siberian maple (*Acer ginnala*) can stand in for the Japanese maple; crabapples (*Malus*) of many varieties can substitute for the flowering cherries;

birch (*Betula*) or even aspen (*Populus tremuloides*) can play the role of crapemyrtle and stewartia. But the last substitution is a stretch, and we are ignoring the floral display.

Finding stand-ins for the azaleas presents a much greater problem. If we ignore the requirement that the replacement be evergreen, *Daphne ×burkwoodii*, or *Daphne ×burkwoodii* 'Carol Mackie', or a short, neat mockorange cultivar such as *Philadelphus* 'Miniature Snowflake' or *Philadelphus* 'Galahad' might do, choices that replace color with fragrance. Dwarf, shrubby members of the genus *Prunus*, such as the dwarf flowering almond (*Prunus glandulosa*), will provide an earlier and shorter display. Even the bush cinquefoils, such as the white *Potentilla fruticosa* 'Abbottswood' or the creamy yellow *Potentilla fruticosa* 'Daydawn', could be used and would extend the flower show well into summer. Unfortunately, the winter aspect of all these replacements is far from that of the azaleas.

If you are willing to trade a bit of the spring flower show for a bit of evergreen winter foliage, holly (*Ilex*) or grapeholly (*Mahonia aquifolium*) might be considered. Even a hardy boxwood (*Buxus*) could be used, forgoing notable bloom or berries and seasonal change altogether. Even a rough approximation of this garden will be worth the reach—it is that satisfying.

Plate 114. Japanese garden at the U.S. National Arboretum, Washington, D.C.

Seventeen Mile Drive

Along the coast of Monterey, California, the famed Seventeen Mile Drive winds its way along some of the poshest property in the state. Here, overlooking the Pacific Ocean or in sight of it from the hills across the road, multimillion-dollar estates testify to the power that wealth has in usurping uniquely scenic tracts of land for private use. Although ostentation is the style of first choice, every expression of taste that money can buy is to be seen along this remarkable stretch of highway. Occasionally, money is placed at the service of art with extraordinary effect, as we see in a hillside garden that uses a modern interpretation of traditional Japanese landscape principles (Plate 115).

The garden surrounds one of the more modest mansions in the area, a ranch-style home that leaves most of the lot free. Monterey cypress (*Cupressus macrocarpa*) frames the garden on the sides and along the back. A superbly shaped pine and a stone lantern acknowledge the debt to the oriental vision. Except for a couple of chest-high spreading junipers and some massive, pale gray boulders, the remaining planting consists of an undulating sea of spreading, low-growing junipers. That is all there is to it; that is all that is needed.

Except for a dry landscape (a garden of stone and gravel with no plants), this is the most carefree of all designs. After the first year or so, no supplemental water is needed, and given the right cultivar, the junipers will need little pruning to maintain the right height and shape. Planted through a weed-barrier fabric that permits the passage of air, water, and nutrients, weeding chores would be non-existent, although junipers planted closely enough will inhibit most weeds even without the barrier fabric.

This landscape may seem severe to some, but to us it is a strong design for which the beauty lies in its clarity and uncluttered vision. While it is distinctly a garden, distinctly set off from its surroundings, it does reflect the natural scenery of Monterey. Near the coast, pure stands of Monterey cypress are sheared flat by the offshore winds, and viewed from a distance, younger stands knit into a contiguous carpet of green, not unlike this hillside of juniper.

As powerful and evocative as it is, some might criticize this design as being too static and too simple to sustain their interest throughout the year. They may feel that this garden design is too set, and tampering with it in any way would dilute its effect; they may feel that this is a garden for non-gardeners. There is some truth to these criticisms, but one could replace the pine with a more complicated planting, perhaps a grove of trees with an understory of flowering shrubs. This would add some seasonal interest and a modest area to putter around in, although the integrity of the design would suffer a bit. On the other hand, those looking for a garden design of maximum impact involving the least amount of maintenance may see this as an ideal model.

Plate 115. Oceanside Japanese garden along Seventeen Mile Drive, Monterey, California.

Golden Gate to Japan

Golden Gate is the strait joining San Francisco Bay to the Pacific Ocean, molten gold in the setting sun. Golden Gate is the audacious more-red-than-gold suspension bridge linking San Francisco to Sausalito, a masterpiece of engineering and design. And Golden Gate is San Francisco's renowned city park, attracting visitors from around the world. The grand old park, reaching inland from the Pacific Ocean, houses an aquarium, a museum of natural history, a museum of art, a grand glasshouse, and an arboretum with an extraordinarily diverse display of plant habitats. None of these attractions is more popular than the Japanese garden. Within its fenced enclosure is a dry landscape, an exquisite tea garden, and a Buddhist monastery garden. But the most glorious feature of all may be the lake garden (Plate 116).

Although the design of the lake garden is convincingly Japanese, certain elements in the design are not at all traditional. The section pictured here features a bank of *Crocosmia* in full bloom in April, setting raucous orange blossoms against bright green foliage. A bit much for traditionalists perhaps, but undeniably effective. Nor is the bronze crane, attractive as it is, likely to be found nesting in a traditional Japanese garden; but in this setting, it seems right at home and, paradoxically, contributes to the oriental character of the garden. It even complements the gangling grace of the tree on the island next to it—the tree too has spindly stilt legs and leans over the water.

As we move away from this section of the pond garden, the bank incorporates more of the features that we expect: clipped boxwood and azaleas, Japanese iris in clumps at the water's edge, an occasional cherry tree, highly trained pines, red-lacquered bridges and other structures, and of course several stone lanterns. It is all superbly composed and flows together seamlessly. Harmonious diversity—a challenge to the skills of the best designer. When successful, as it is here, what a delight it is, generating excitement and interest for us along every step of the path.

Can we imagine a counterpart of this section in a private setting or on the grounds of some public building? Absolutely! The scale is certainly appropriate, and the overall effect is quite contemporary. Adapting the planting to climates colder than zone 9, however, does require some alterations. We were not able to get close enough to the trees on the peninsula to identify them, but if the one with the rough bark and single trunk were removed, we would not miss it. On the other hand, the multi-trunked tree further back is an essential part of the composition. We think that a pagoda dogwood (*Cornus alternifolia*) would be perfect. Grown with several stems, its horizontal branching pattern would complement the shoreline, the purple-red color of the leaves in autumn would brighten that season, and even the 3-in (7.5 cm) flat cymes of tiny creamy white blossoms would be welcome in the spring—the whole yearlong show would be varied and quietly beautiful. In spite of its origin in the southeastern United States, pagoda dogwood is hardy through zone 4. The flowering dogwoods (*C. florida*

Plate 116. Japanese garden in Golden Gate Park, San Francisco, California.

and *C. kousa*) would also be magnificent in this application, but neither is as hardy, and neither is quite as tolerant of moist soils.

Other choices are equally likely to satisfy. Shadblow (*Amelanchier*) offers several species and varieties that are readily grown as multi-stemmed trees of modest height. Brilliant red-orange fall color is their trademark, but the early panicles of white blossoms are also welcome. The berries that follow the flowers are relished by birds and beasts; new selections vie with blueberries for taste. Some shadblows are hardy in zone 3. A flowering crabapple (*Malus*) would also do nicely. Modern cultivars vary in size from 6 ft (1.8 m) to over 20 ft (6 m) and come in a variety of forms, from weeping to fastigiate. Those that have a spreading habit with undulating branches are probably the most suitable. Cultivars that offer fall color are available, and many are resistant to disease. Cherries, plums, and apricots (*Prunus*) might also be considered, but most are more sensitive to excessive moisture at the roots than either the shadblows or the crabapples.

If you can do without the spring blossoms, consider cultivars of the Japanese maple (*Acer palmatum*) and the fullmoon maple (*A. japonicum*): small trees that are perfect for this type of garden, trees that offer a variety of delicate leaf shapes and unsurpassed fall color, trees that are easily grown with multiple stems. Unfortunately, few are reliably hardy in zone 4, and some cannot be trusted in zone 5. In places where more cold hardiness is needed, the Siberian maple (*Acer ginnala*) is a worthy alternative.

Accompanying the trees on the island are azaleas and ferns. Depending on the species, ferns are available for use in zones 2 through 10. Stand-ins will have to be considered for the azaleas for zones colder than zone 5; maybe some dwarf plum or almond (*Prunus*) will do. If flowers are not essential, boxwood (*Buxus*), holly (*Ilex*), or some low-growing conifer, such as *Chamaecyparis*, *Juniperus*, or *Picea*, will do nicely. But nothing will work quite as well as azaleas.

For the background, selections of *Crocosmia* can be found that are hardy in zones 5 through 9; their suitability for zone 4 has been highly exaggerated. For this and colder zones, some of the alternatives to azaleas suggested above might prove suitable. If you wanted something different and seasonally spectacular, a dwarf cultivar of the shasta daisy (*Chrysanthemum* ×*superbum*) would do, or a pink or white cultivar of *Chrysanthemum weyrichii*. However, it is hard to find a substitute that can match the brilliant color and distinctive form of the *Crocosmia*.

As always, it is the overall layout of the garden that gives it its essential character, and not the specific choice of plant material. Even furnished with other plants, this would be a remarkable and memorable garden.

A Reflection of Japan Across the Pacific

The maritime climate of Seattle, Washington, is a fair approximation to that of Japan. In the moist air and moderate temperatures of the Pacific Northwest, the plants of the traditional Japanese gardens find a home away from home. Rhododendrons, maples and pines, flowering cherries and flowering apricots, hollies, and boxwoods are raised here commercially for sale in the United States and abroad. Bamboos, ferns, hostas, and Japanese iris grow as vigorously here as anywhere. A sizable Japanese population preserves its traditional culture, including its heritage of the horticultural arts. So it is not surprising to find a large and magnificent Japanese-style garden as part of the Washington Park Arboretum in Seattle, Washington (Plate 117).

The garden is designed around a large lake, on which islands and a meandering shoreline provide a variety of sites and microclimates for plants. Ferns, primulas, and Japanese iris march down to the water's edge. On higher and drier ground, *Rhododendron*, *Pieris*, and *Kalmia* contribute foliage mass and fine texture to the design—beautiful even when not in flower. Weeping willows (*Salix*), birch (*Betula*), and flowering cherries (*Prunus*) lift the design high above the water. Yew (*Taxus*), hemlock (*Tsuga*), *Cryptomeria*, upright junipers (*Juniperus*), *Chamaecyparis*, and other conifers create a backdrop of dense, mostly dark evergreen foliage.

Smaller trees, mainly Japanese and fullmoon maples (*Acer palmatum* and *A. japonicum*), carry the design through the intermediate heights. Imagine what color they bring to the autumn landscape: subtle gold, brilliant orange, incandescent red, and even deep purple light up this garden, exchanging serenity for excitement. The size and variety of leaf shapes and the diversity of plant forms bring elements of texture, line, and mass into the picture.

And, of course, there are pines—Japanese black pines (*Pinus thunbergii*) and Japanese white pines (*P. parviflora*)—located on the islands and right at the shore of the lake, often set off against massive boulders. The trees are pruned and shaped with a bonsai master's skill to interact with the stone and the water. Often they are trained to lean over the lake, imparting tension and static energy to an otherwise tranquil scene. These pines are but chest high or smaller, but the energy they communicate far exceeds their size.

The landscape includes the typical teahouse and viewing pavilion, wooden bridges, and stone lanterns to emphasize the Japanese character of the garden, but none of these is needed. The oriental influence is quite apparent; the garden is richly Japanese in its controlled use of color and form, in the exquisite refinement and balance of the overall design, and most of all, in its deep sensitivity to the canons of nature.

The scale of this garden is far too large to be accommodated in a private landscape or even on the grounds of most public and corporate buildings; but if we focus on a portion of the scene, ignoring most of the large trees that define the background, then there is a great deal of inspiration and a great number of ideas to be gleaned from it. For example, pines and maples of modest size provide an inexhaustible source of materials for this type of garden. How well they associate with each other, with stone, and with water. Such delicious contrasts—evergreen against deciduous, deep green needle foliage barely moving in the wind played against the light green maple foliage alive in every breeze. Small pines and maples suitable for this kind of interplay can be found in almost every temperate region, although from zones 5 through 7 one cannot do better than to use the plants found in this example from Washington Park.

Plate 117. Reflection of Japan in Washington Park Arboretum, Seattle, Washington.

Of course, this is not a maintenance-free landscape. Wherever you find such perfect balance between diverse plant forms, such perfect integration of plants, stone, and water, such perfect control of individual shapes, skilled gardeners have been devoting time and effort to create it and maintain it. But an extensive rose garden or vegetable garden would require even more care, and while this garden neither titillates the nose nor supplies the belly, it nurtures the spirit as well as any.

A Japanese Garden in the Mile-High City

The high-plains climate of Denver, Colorado, is far from the maritime climate of Japan. Here, in the mile-high city, gardeners are severely limited in their use of traditional landscape plants of Japan. Azaleas, flowering cherries, bamboos, and Japanese maples have been known to survive in Denver, but only those made of the sturdiest stuff, and even these survive only with the help of dedicated gardeners made of even sturdier stuff.

A mile above sea level is a mile less of atmosphere to moderate the sun. Moisture, when it comes (Denver gets about 15 in [38 cm] of precipitation annually), can be hail, sleet, or snow as often as rain. In winter, the soil alternately freezes and thaws; sunny days with temperatures above 50°F (10°C) alternate with days well below 0°F (–18°C). During summer, temperatures regularly go above 90°F (32°C) with little humidity and no clouds. Winds in excess of 50 miles per hour (83 km/hr) can occur during any season. Don't

misunderstand us, we love it here, although the traditional garden plants of Japan must have a different view.

So, given all the restrictions that the climate imposes, it is rather surprising to find a superb, large-scale Japanese-style garden near the center of the city, but such a garden exists, complete with pond, islands, streams, and teahouse. Shofu-en, The Garden of Pine Wind, is part of the Denver Botanic Gardens. Designed by the Japanese landscape architect Koichi Kawana with the assistance of experienced high-plains horticulturists, it is a garden of necessary compromises, not in beauty, but only in the plants used to achieve the result.

There are a few risky choices. Flowering cherries (*Prunus*), gifts from the Japanese ambassador, survive the winter wrapped in a multi-layered overcoat of straw and cloth blankets; Japanese maples (*Acer palmatum*) hunker under the protection of a pavilion. The moss on the banks of the pond and streams is not Japanese, but Irish and Scotch (*Sagina subulata*). Clumps of Japanese iris (*Iris kaempferi*), planted in buckets buried in the soil, are seen along the banks of the stream and pond. Most of the trees are pines; Japanese black and Japanese white pines (*Pinus thunbergii* and *P. parviflora*) are represented, but many are ponderosa pines (*P. ponderosa*), a tree that is native to this area. Pruning and shaping has given these trees ancient and heroic forms that suggest large-scale bonsai. Every year, the candles of the pines are shortened and the needles pruned to keep the trees in scale and maintain their shape. Mugo pines (*P. mugo*), low- to medium-height junipers (*Juniper-*

us), and evergreen barberries (*Berberis*) play the role of azaleas for foliage mass. It's a traditional style Japanese stroll garden using non-traditional plants—quite convincing and deeply satisfying.

The section we want to focus on is an island (Plate 118) that is capable of being enjoyed as a self-contained landscape or as an integral part of the overall composition. The primary feature of the island is a pair of European white birches (*Betula pendula*). No more elegant tree can grace a pond or lake; none has a more striking bark; and none has a more graceful weeping form. Willows and even weeping flowering cherries are coarse by comparison. The character of these trees, their supreme refinement, is in perfect harmony with the Japanese aesthetic, but these trees from Europe are never seen in the traditional Japanese garden.

With birch as the central element of the island's design and with boulders to define its shore, many options are suitable for completing the picture. Water-loving iris, such as Japanese iris (*Iris kaempferi*), *I. laevigata*, *I. pseudacorus*, and several others, depending on your taste and the local climate, will be perfect along the shore between the boulders. Junipers intermixed with azaleas or some dwarf variety of the doublefile viburnum, like 'Shasta' (*Viburnum plicatum* var. *tomentosum* 'Shasta'), will work nicely under the birch. All these are shade tolerant. In warmer climates, a dwarf, shrubby crapemyrtle (*Lagerstroemia indica*) or a small clone of a small magnolia (*Magnolia liliiflora* or *M. stellata*) might be used.

Of course, there is one minor restriction: you have to have an island, or at least a peninsula. On the other hand, this landscape scene need not be surrounded by water; sand or gravel or even grass can suggest water, as the Japanese have shown us. Then we can each have our own island. Now that is a luxury.

Plate 118. Shofu-en, Japanese garden in the Denver Botanic Gardens, Denver, Colorado.

A Buddhist Stone Garden Indoors

In an ordinary office building near an ordinary shopping mall in Boulder, Colorado, is an extraordinary Japanese garden (Plate 119), the inspiration of Kanjuro Shibata Sensei, a twentieth-generation bow maker to the Emperor of Japan. Enter this building and you enter a different time and a different place.

The garden, lit by skylights two stories above, stretches half the length of the first floor. It is a dry landscape using only stone and gravel, yet the imagery evoked is rich in water features. Standing in the viewing pavilion (from where our photograph was taken), you are led to imagine that the water has its source in the far right-hand corner. There, an upright grouping of large boulders suggests a distant mountain, from the heights of which a stream emerges, gains in volume to become a river, and flows into a pond. The river continues under a bridge made of tree limb sections with bark intact, and empties into a larger pond. All this is implied by the careful placement of stones and gravel—movement implied by a completely static design.

The construction of this garden presented special problems. For one, additional joists had to be installed under the floor to support the massive tonnage of boulders being brought in. The rock itself also presented a problem. The kind of dark gray, river-polished rock that Sensei envisioned in his design can be found in only a few places, none near Colorado, and transporting such rock in the quantity needed would have been too costly. So boulders found in the Poudre River in northern Colorado were used instead. Duller and lighter in color than wanted, they were given a clear glaze to create the desired effect. And the construction of the garden was not without risks to the building and to the engineers. At one stage of the installation, a boulder broke loose of the hoist, came crashing to the floor, and seemed destined to make its way to Japan. Luckily, the joists held, and construction continued.

Unfortunately, Sensei's masterpiece cannot be easily transferred to other sites. The scale is too large, the costs for material and installation too high, and more importantly, the tone of the garden might strike some as too austere, too serious, and maybe too somber. Some will argue that once in place, such a garden allows no freedom to garden; that the garden is too static and unresponsive to the seasons; that the garden is so abstract that it relegates its creator to anonymity.

Yet, how appropriate the design is as a complement to modern architecture, to grace the alcove of some corporate headquarters or some public building. It has practical virtues as well. No plants means no watering and no problem with lighting. The design will never look tired, shabby, or overgrown. Maintenance is minimal.

Certainly, this is not a garden for all tastes. Nor is it a garden for the casual viewer. This garden was designed to be much more than merely decorative. It has the power to move you, and it can do so like no other that we know of. It's a masterpiece.

Plate 119. Indoor Buddhist stone garden, Boulder, Colorado.

GEOGRAPHICAL INDEX

INDEX OF PLANT NAMES